BERRIES

To

Magic and Tabitha, with all our love

THE ENGLISH KITCHEN

BERRIES

GROWING AND COOKING

JANE MCMORLAND HUNTER
AND
SALLY HUGHES

PROSPECT BOOKS
2016

This edition published in 2016 in Great Britain and the USA by
Prospect Books at 26 Parke Road, London, SW13 9NG

British Library Cataloguing in Publication Data:
A catalogue entry for this book is available from the British Library.

ISBN 978-1-909248-45-8

Printed by the Gutenberg Press Ltd., Malta.

TABLE OF CONTENTS

INTRODUCTION

Honeyberries

I t is all too easy to take berries for granted. They are gaily flown around the world, crushed, freeze dried, drowned in sugary syrup, and their flavourings are hijacked by the most unlikely of foods – stretchy gums, fluorescent ice-lollies, and more. We should revere the humble berry, and learn to grow our own, like our ancestors. Since prehistoric times they have been an important source of food and medicine; while the men hunted, the women gathered, learning by experience which were the best berries. Ancient Greeks, Romans, Native Americans and the nomads of Central Asia all recognized the importance of these fruits; they deserve more attention and respect than we often give them.

Many berries have prestigious histories; raspberries are red because Zeus' nursemaid Ida, pricked her finger on the thorns, the Druids regarded cranberries as sacred and Native American tribal elders recounted how the Great Spirit sent 'star berries' or blueberries as we know them, to ease children's hunger during a famine. Shakespeare's Falstaff recognizes an abundance of blackberries ('If reasons were as plentiful as blackberries…'), Mark Twain immortalized huckleberries in his novel of 1884 and writers as diverse as Tolstoy and Simone de Beauvoir have offered advice on making jam.

In the kitchen berries are all round performers, enhancing sweet and savoury dishes alike. They can be preserved as jams, jellies, curds or chutneys and bottled in sugar or alcohol. Cakes, biscuits and puddings are all better for the addition of a few berries and in some, such as Eton Mess, fools and clafoutis the berries are the stars.

As all berries are delicate, they are going to benefit hugely from the few feet they will travel from your garden or hedgerow, rather than the miles they would have had to travel to a shop. Many berries can be harvested wild and, although you obviously have to be careful to identify them correctly, many of the best childhood memories centre round red-stained fingers and a basket of freshly foraged fruit. Wild blackberries may not be as large or glossy as their shop-sold cousins, but they have far more flavour and are much more fun to obtain.

Another way to get top quality fruit is to grow your own. Whether your kitchen garden consists of a couple of window boxes or a complete allotment, berries are an easy and invaluable addition. Mostly perennials or shrubs, they will give structure to the area, enchanting blossom in spring, a bountiful harvest you would have trouble buying and, in many cases, beautiful autumn colour and brilliant stems in winter. Growing your own berries is one of those areas of kitchen gardening that is definitely an economy; buying the initial plants may seem costly, but most live for years and even in season, berries tend to be expensive.

Strawberries, in particular, may look enticing on the shelves but, unless you are very lucky, will almost certainly be pretty tasteless. Some fruits, such as alpine strawberries are very hard to buy. They are incredibly easy to grow, will fit into any space and taste amazing.

Raspberries are also expensive to buy and as they turn squishy if you wash them, you really do want to know that they have been grown without the addition of anything you would prefer not to eat. Cultivating your own organically is the obvious and simple solution. By planting summer and autumn fruiting varieties you can have perfect fruit from mid summer right through to autumn.

Blackberries can be a bit rampant, but even here there is a strong argument in favour of growing your own. With a firm hand the long canes are easily kept under control and many of the commercially

available varieties are thornless, reasonably compact, turn beautiful colours in autumn and look lovely twining along a wall or fence. Many of the hybrid brambles are also worth growing, mainly because they rarely appear in shops or even farmers' markets. Tayberries, loganberries and boysenberries all have their own individual charms. As well as delicious fruit, many have good looks; Japanese wineberries have brilliant red stems with red bristles and many bramble cultivars have white-bloomed stems in winter. The huge range of hybrids available means that you can almost certainly find one that will be happy whatever conditions you have.

Blueberries, cranberries and lingonberries all have reputations as superfoods. This is undoubtedly well-deserved and the perfect way to get the best from any fruit is to cultivate your own; no air miles, no refrigeration and no chemicals. These berries demand damp, acidic soil, but apart from that they are simple and rewarding to grow, with blueberries giving good autumn colour and cranberries and lingonberries providing evergreen structure to the garden all year round. Goji berries, which have been cultivated for centuries in China, even having their own festival, are also a superfood and well worth growing. Other more unusual berries such as haskap or honeyberries (an edible honeysuckle), huckleberries and mulberries are also worth considering.

Many ornamental plants have edible berries and your crop need not be confined to the working part of a garden (assuming you have the luxury of sufficient space for such divisions). Hawthorns, barberries and checkerberries will increase the beauty of your garden as well as providing you with a bountiful harvest.

The first part of this book tells the story of berries in history, literature and folklore. Their many health benefits are then described, followed by two sections on obtaining your berries: foraging and growing. We describe which are the best berries to look out for, which to avoid and give clear instructions for growing a huge range of berries, which can be used by experienced or novice gardeners alike. Lastly, and perhaps most importantly, come the recipes; over seventy ways to use berries in your kitchen, from Cranberry Roast

Ham to Raspberry Brownies and Blueberry Pancakes to Sloe Gin.

Botanists define berries in a way that would leave most lay people baffled, the consequence of which is that tomatoes are berries and strawberries are not. This book works on the premise that if it looks like a berry and tastes like a berry then it probably should be called a berry. We hope that we have included all the berries that readers would expect to find and also introduced them to a few new or unusual ones.

THE STORY OF THE BERRY

Names of plants and surviving scraps of belief show how many English kinds were associated with elf or fairy, or devil, or with that ultimate being of superstition, the poor witch.

(Geoffrey Grigson, *The Englishman's Flora*)

Man originally depended entirely on hunting and gathering; he picked what he could as and when nature made it available. Berries have grown wild in Britain, northern Europe and much of North America since the retreat of the Ice Age and have probably been eaten since Neolithic times. As people became more settled they domesticated many foods, growing berries in the fertile waste areas round their settlements.

Berries were an important part of man's diet for many hundreds of years, but they were originally collected, rather than cultivated. This was partly because the berries were abundant and the time and effort needed to grow them domestically didn't seem to give a marked improvement in flavour. The Romans used berries to add flavour to many of their dishes, but few were grown in Roman gardens.

As the Middle Ages progressed, gardens became more ornate and berries were grown for medicinal and food purposes. In 1573 Thomas

Tusser wrote *Five Hundreth Points of Good Husbandry*, a rhyming manual which became enormously popular. His instructions for September include:

> The Barbary, Respis* and Goosebery too,
> looke now to be planted as other things doo:
> The Goosebery, Respis, and Roses, al three,
> with Strawberies under them trimly agree.

(*Respis are raspberries)

Herbals abound with references to berries, both practical and fanciful. John Gerard's *Great Herball* of 1578 contains numerous references to berries, both medicinal and horticultural. Strictly speaking, this herbal should be credited to the Belgian botanist Rembert Dodoens; Gerard simply completed a translation of the work. He added a few misidentifications and inaccuracies of his own, such as sweepingly stating that raspberries were rarely to be found growing in the wild, but he had judged his market well and a little inaccuracy has never hampered book sales; it was an instant success. Almost a hundred years later, in 1653 Nicolas Culpeper, an apothecary, published his *Complete Herbal*. He was convinced that the body should be treated as a whole and described occult properties as well as medicinal ones. He said of barberries 'The berries are as good as the bark and more pleasing; they get a man a good stomach to his victuals, by strengthening the attractive faculty which is under Mars'. Barberries were a classic example of the like-for-like principle which forms the basis of the *Doctrine of Signatures*; a plant which resembles an ailment can be used to cure it. In this case the yellow inner bark and roots of the barberry tree were, hopelessly, used to treat any disease which caused a yellowing of the skin.

Illuminated manuscripts and tapestries are frequently adorned with borders of trailing berries, although they appear in still life paintings less often than one might expect. Perhaps they were just too fragile and grapes made more robust subjects.

Berries disguised the questionable quality of much of the meat people ate and in Victorian Britain berries livened up the stodgy diets of many people; pies, bread, potatoes and cheap cuts of meat or fish all benefitted from the addition of a few berries. Rather surprisingly though, many early cookery books have few berry recipes compared with pears, apples and quinces. This is probably because until the eighteenth century raw fruit was regarded with suspicion and felt to be potentially dangerous to one's health. This was largely based on the fact that when there was a glut people tended to overeat and make themselves ill. Strawberries and cream seem to be one of the exceptions to this, possibly because strawberries in those days were so small that it was hard to over-indulge on them. Raspberries, elder flowers and berries and gooseberries appear in the cookbooks of the seventeenth and early eighteenth centuries, but mostly in recipes for wine, vinegar or jams and jellies. Gooseberries appear as fools and with chicken in Tudor recipes but these were cooked dishes and would have been regarded as safer. Barberries, myrtles and juniper berries appear more commonly than they do now as these berries were regarded as beneficial to health.

In North America the Native Americans used berries as an important part of their diet. They were eaten fresh, but also crushed, or dried and pounded, and made into cakes to eat during winter. Pemmican, possibly best known as the food of Arctic explorers, originated in North America. It is a mixture of dried meat, melted fat and berries, the word coming from the Cree *pimi* meaning fat. The assumption is that the European settlers took advantage of this knowledge and made berries a major part of their diet too. In fact not that many did. Most wanted their own crops and agricultural skill to feed themselves and their families, foraging was for natives. They ate the local berries and adapted some native recipes but not to any great extent.

BILBERRIES

Bilberries gained their name from the Danish *bollebar* meaning a dark berry. Their other common English name, hurtleberry, refers to the dark purple colour from a bruise or hurt. West Country words frequently add a 'w' and from this we get whortleberry.

Traditionally in many European countries, the Sunday nearest to 1st August was set aside for harvesting bilberries; Fraughan Sunday is still celebrated in parts of Ireland and Whort Sunday in the West Country. In the past, children were given days off school to collect the berries in return for a few pennies, but few modern children can be so easily bribed (or allowed the time away). The Gaelic festival of Lughnasadh which takes place on 1st August is also a traditional time to collect bilberries. This festival marks the beginning of the harvest season and the success or otherwise of the bilberry collection is seen as a harbinger of later harvests.

Jane Grigson tells of an eighteenth century traveller who sneered at the fruits, 'The taste of them, to me, is not very agreeable; but they are much esteemed by the inhabitants, who eat them with their milk'.

Thomas Hardy called them black-hearts, a common nineteenth century name and wrote about them in *The Return of the Native*, where picking the berries leads a country lad to see more than he should have.

BLACKBERRIES AND BRAMBLES

Brambles (coming from the Ango-Saxon *bremel*) have always been regarded as a good wild food. Part of the rose family, they are native to Europe and the temperate regions of North and South America, Asia and Australia. Pips were found in the stomach of a Neolithic body preserved in clay on the Essex coast. They are a huge family of berries, all of which are edible and most of which are delicious. Pliny the Elder (AD 23-79), in his *Natural History* recognizes their value: 'Nature did not intend even brambles to have only harmful purposes and so she provided them with blackberries which are food even for men'. Horticulturally, he says that it was from brambles that we learnt how to propagate plants by layering. The way the stems bent down to the earth and easily took root provided an easy lesson to copy.

Brambles all grow on long trailing stems known as lawyers because of the trouble you will have escaping once ensnared in their thorny grip. However, not everyone dislikes the trailing stems and Walt Whitman, in his poem *The Leaves of Grass* has them adorning the parlours of heaven. The poet Thomas Woolner also used this thorny grip to his advantage:

> We thread a copse where frequent bramble spray
> With loose obtrusion from the side roots stray,
> And force sweet pauses on our walk;
> I lift one with my foot, and talk
> About its leaves and stalk.
>
> Or maybe that some thorn or prickly stem
> Will take a prisoner her long garments' hem;
> To disentangle it I kneel,
> Oft wounding more than I can heal;
> It makes her laugh, my zeal.

> (From *My Beautiful Lady Nelly Dale*)

In the Old Testament the bramble ruled the kingdom of the flora and it may have been the thorns in Christ's Crown of Thorns. The long stems were traditionally twined round coffins to keep the devil out. Geoffrey Grigson in *An Englishman's Flora* has a delightful explanation for the snagging thorns: in an Elizabethan folk tale, a cormorant, a bat and a bramble became business partners. Their plan was to export sheep's wool, but the ship sank on its first voyage and ever since cormorants dive to try to recover the wool, bats hide by day to avoid their creditors and brambles collect sheep's wool on their thorns.

Historically brambles were valued for food and medicine. Culpeper's *Herbal* states 'the berries or flowers are a powerful remedy against the poison of most venomous serpents' and it was believed that if a person passed under an arch where a blackberry had rooted at either end, they would be cured of any disease. At the beginning of the twentieth century, the Royal Navy used the high level of vitamin C in loganberries, a blackberry-raspberry cross, to prevent scurvy. The Romans used blackberry juice as hair dye and later it was used in navy blue and indigo dyes for cloth. Victorian servants dipped their black worsted stockings in blackberry juice to intensify the colour when they started to fade.

Brambles are so prolific that for hundreds of years no one bothered to cultivate them. Thomas Hill in *The Gardener's Labyrinth* of 1577 recommends blackberries, along with gooseberries and barberries, as a natural hedge, but makes no mention of the berries. In literature blackberrying is a common theme with Sylvia Plath describing 'A blackberry alley, going down in hooks,' (from *Blackberrying*), and Seamus Heaney tasting the first fruit, 'At first, just one, a glossy purple clot / Among others, red, green, hard as a knot. / You ate that first one and its flesh was sweet / Like thickened wine' (from *Blackberry-Picking*).

BLACKTHORN or SLOES

Tradition has it that witches' staves were made of blackthorn. The black stems of the trees seem eminently suitable for this. The spikes are a contender for Christ's Crown of Thorns, along with brambles, hawthorn and most other prickly stems. More prosaically, the stems are used for walking sticks. We may use the berries to flavour gin, but the ancient herbalists recommended them for almost all complaints relating to the blood.

The blossom comes in early spring and often coincides with a cold spell, giving rise to the phrase 'a blackthorn winter'. Christina

Rossetti describes this beautifully in her poem *Endure Hardness*:

A cold wind stirs the blackthorn
To burgeon and to blow,
Besprinkling half-green hedges
With flakes and sprays of snow.
Thro' coldness and thro' keenness,
Dear hearts, take comfort so:
Somewhere or other doubtless
These make the blackthorn blow.

BLUEBERRIES

Native Americans call these berries star berries because on each berry the calyx forms a five-pointed star. There is a folk tale which tells that at times of starvation the Great Spirit sent the star berries down from the night of heaven to feed the children. Most were dried in the sun, pounded into a powder and used to flavour stews and porridge. They were popular with the early settlers who adapted Sautauthig, one of the native recipes. It was a simple mixture of blueberries, cracked corn and water, to which the settlers added milk, butter and sugar, possibly eating it at the first Thanksgiving feast.

These are the wild berries of North America which have been cultivated in Britain for little more than a hundred years. In 1912 Robert Frost, living in England, but homesick for his previous home in New Hampshire, wrote of blueberries 'as big as your thumb'. He goes on to describe the bloom as 'The blue's but a mist from the breath of the wind, a tarnish that goes at the touch of a hand' (from *Blueberries*).

The blueberry is the official fruit of both Maine and Nova Scotia, often resulting in acrimonious commercial rivalry between the two states.

CLOUDBERRIES

The name of this berry probably comes from the Old English word *clud*, meaning hill, as they are usually found growing on high moorland, not from the more romantic thought that these hilltops are usually swathed in cloud. The Latin name, *Rubus chamaemorus,* comes from the Greek *chamai* meaning dwarf and *morus*, a mulberry. They are mostly a wild plant, but the berries are so highly prized in Norway that in the 1990s the Northernberries Research Project was set up to cultivate the berries in Norway, Sweden, Finland and Scotland. They are a useful crop as they grow where little else can survive.

Their literary claim to fame is that the writer Alexander Pushkin is reputed to have asked for cloudberries while on his deathbed. Some sources give the berries as blackberries, but cloudberries would certainly have grown round St Petersburg and seem a more likely choice.

CRANBERRIES

These berries were originally called *samolus* by the Druids and later marsh worts or fen berries because of the areas in which they were found. They may have become cranberries because cranes liked the fruits and built their nests nearby or because the pink flowers resemble the bird's head. Another name is the bounceberry as they bounce when ripe. In the States commercial pickers developed a machine which dropped the berries, allowing the firm, good ones to bounce onto a conveyor belt, while the squishy ones fell into a bin. Henry David Thoreau described them as 'small waxen gems, pendants of the meadow grass, pearly and red' (*Walden*).

A Bronze Age tomb in Jutland, Denmark contained a clay jug with the remains of a drink made from cranberries, wheat, bog myrtle and honey. Although cranberries grow wild in Europe and have been eaten since ancient times they never gained much popularity there and the North American fruits are the ones which have become popular worldwide. They were one of the wild fruits that the early settlers heavily relied on. They had known cranberries from Europe, but the American fruits were much larger and easier to harvest. They were not mentioned as part of the first Thanksgiving feast in 1621, but as the settlers knew them from Europe they may simply have been collected from the wild and added without being recorded. Of course now no Christmas or Thanksgiving table is complete without a ruby dish of cranberry sauce. In 1677 the colonists sent ten barrels of cranberries to Charles II. Much to the king's fury, the colonists had minted their own coins and they hoped the berries would mollify the monarch.

Cranberries have never really taken off as a commercial crop in Britain partly because there isn't that much suitable land but they are a major crop in North America and Canada, with most berries being made into juice or dried and a small amount sold fresh in autumn. The huge fields are flooded to make harvesting easier and are a truly remarkable sight.

ELDER

The name elder comes from the Anglo-Saxon *aeld* meaning fire. The older branches are easily hollowed and could be used as bellows to get a fire started. According to need, they can also be used as pea shooters, blow pipes or whistles. Culpeper says, 'I hold it needless to write any description of this, since every boy that plays with a pop-gun will not mistake another tree instead of elder'. The Latin name *Sambucus*, comes from sambuca, a Roman musical instrument. Care should be taken with all these as the wood is toxic and not really something you want to put in your mouth for too long.

All parts of the elder have been credited with medicinal properties and a host of myths surround the tree. Christ's Cross was made of elder wood and Judas was said to have hanged himself from an elder tree. A traditional Scottish verse says it all:

Bour-tree*, bour-tree, crookit rung,
Never straight, and never strong,
Ever bush, and never tree
Since our Lord was nailed t'ye.

(*In Scotland the elder is called the bour-tree)

Elder trees are said to protect a house from evil spirits and lightning, but should not be felled as they are home to the Elder or Earth Mother who will then take her revenge. It was also believed that putting the wood on a fire would release the devil into your home. This latter superstition is entirely sensible as burning elder wood releases cyanide, which will indeed harm you. In Ireland the wood cannot be used for boat building. The trees were often planted near graves to protect the body and flowering would indicate that the soul was at peace.

Elderberries were used by the Romans as hair dye and later to treat dropsy. According to Gerard, they also helped with weight loss: 'The seeds contained within the berries dried are good for such that have the Dropsie, and such as are too fat and would faine be leaner, if they be taken in a morning to the quantitie of a dram with wine for a certain space'. The flowers, distilled in water were used to cure ulcers, bloodshot eyes and shaking caused by the palsy. According to Vicomte de Mauduit in *They Can't Ration These*, a book published in 1940 on how to make the most of natural ingredients, the flowers could also be used to treat freckles: 'Pick the flowers when they are in full bloom and soak 2 handfuls of them in a quart of boiling water. Allow to stand till luke-warm, then strain and wash the face with this lotion.'

Sambuca is made of an infusion of elderberries and anise in alcohol and in Hungary an elderberry brandy is made. Elderberry wine became so popular in Britain at one time that vast orchards were planted in Kent. The juice was often used to bulk up claret or port and in eighteenth-century Portugal it became illegal to cultivate the fruit.

GOJI BERRIES

The name goji is comparatively recent and is a corruption of the Chinese name *gou qi zi*. Before this in Britain it was known as the Chinese wolfberry, the matrimony vine, the Chinese boxthorn, the red medlar or the Duke of Argyll's Tea-tree. This last name supposedly arose from the mislabelling of *Lycium* (goji) and *Thea* (tea) plants which were sent to the Duke's garden at Whitton in Middlesex.

Goji berries are native to the valleys of the Himalayas. When herbalists came to the valleys to visit the healers there, they realized the value of the berries and took plants back to the rest of India, China and Tibet. During the Tang Dynasty (c800 AD) a well was dug at a Buddhist temple which was covered with goji vines. The berries fell into the water and people who regularly drank from the well remained healthy, earning the temple a great reputation. It is likely however, that the goji water was more effective than the prayers.

GOOSEBERRIES

The name gooseberry probably comes from the French word *groseille* which, in turn, stems from the Frankish *krûsil*, meaning crisp berry. Another possibility is that the thorns resemble gorse, which then became corrupted into goose. These berries are eaten both by and with geese; young geese like the berries and gooseberry sauce goes well with the rich meat. One is reminded of poor Jemima Puddle-Duck collecting sage and thyme for dinner with the gentleman with sandy whiskers. Another English name, feaberry, may come from the Old English *theve* meaning thorn.

European gooseberries are native to the Caucasus Mountains and North Africa and now grow wild throughout Europe. American gooseberries are similar plants and grow in most of North America and southern Canada. Gooseberries were first mentioned as cultivated plants in England in thirteenth-century bills of purchase for Edward I's gardens. They were popular in kitchen gardens by the sixteenth century, but mostly for decorative or medicinal purposes. They were recommended, without much success, for victims of the Great Plague in 1665, but then nothing had much success against that plague. The early English name feaberrie, may also refer to the use of the juice in cooling fevers.

They are also known as wineberries; a sparkling gooseberry wine being sometimes passed off as champagne in times of fewer regulations. John Evelyn collected a great many recipes in the seventeenth century, among them one from the architect Sir Christopher Wren for gooseberry wine:

> *To make goosberie wine fr Chris: wren*
> Take goosberies droping ripe next to rottenesse squeeze them
> to mash thick as mustard let it work and be well scumed, tun
> up the cleere and it will ferment again being kept 2 yeare it
> is an excellent wine.

From the mid eighteenth century onwards gooseberry clubs were set up, particularly in the north of England and the Midlands, each trying to grow the largest fruits. At the height of their popularity there were different 3,000 varieties and in 1845 the Gooseberry Growers' Register listed over 170 shows. There was even a Gooseberry Growers' Song written in 1885 with fifteen verses describing many of the best varieties:

> Come all ye jovial gardeners, and listen unto me
> While I relate the different sorts of winning gooseberries
> This famous institution was founded long ago,
> That men might meet and drink and have a gooseberry show.

Mrs Beeton's *Household Management* was first published in 1861, at the height of the gooseberry's popularity and she describes them as a 'useful and wholesome fruit' and goes on to say they 'may occasionally be found in a wild state in some of the eastern counties, although when uncultivated, it is but a very small and inferior berry. The high state of perfection to which it has been here brought, is due to the skill of the English gardeners'. She then gives a number of recipes, including baked and boiled puddings, sauce for mackerel and trifle, along with the more usual fool, compote, jam and jelly.

In 1905 a mildew disease was accidentally introduced from America and the entire European crop was destroyed. New varieties were gradually established by using crosses with mildew-resistant American varieties. In Europe, it was only in Britain that gooseberries became really popular, although there is a Chekhov short story of 1898 called *Gooseberries* in which a man dreams of retiring to a country estate with a gooseberry patch. In France they have never even had a proper name and are simply called redcurrant for mackerel (*groseille de maquereau*).

Gooseberries seem to have entered into sayings more than most other berries. 'Being a gooseberry' or the unwanted third at a couple's meeting is of uncertain origin. It is possible that it is short for gooseberry picker, the idea being that the chaperone would be distracted by picking fruit to allow the loving couple privacy while still preserving respectability. Finding babies under gooseberry bushes may originate from the Victorian meaning of the flower as 'to anticipate' or from the earlier meaning of pubic hair. 'Going gooseberrying' means to steal clothes from a washing line and the 'great gooseberry season' is a newspaper term for a time when there is little news, possibly nothing except the size of the latest crop of fruit.

HAWTHORN

The hawthorn is one of the most magical trees in Western Europe, marking the change from spring to summer, with the common name, May, being used to describe the tree's flowering time. Before the calendar was revised in 1752 and May Day moved forward thirteen days, it is likely that the blossom often coincided with May Day celebrations. The saying 'Cast ne'er a clout ere May is out' almost certainly refers to the blossom rather than the month. The name hawthorn came from the old English *haw*, which means both berry and hedge. *Crategus*, the Latin name, comes from the Greek *kratos* meaning strength and refers to the hardness of the wood.

The most famous hawthorn is the Glastonbury Thorn which is said to have sprouted from the staff of Joseph of Arimathea and flowers on Christmas Day. The staff was reputed to be an offshoot of Christ's Crown of Thorns and when Joseph stuck it in the ground it burst into flower. A variation of the story is that he had the Crown of Thorns with him and that the bush took root from a fragment of that. The bush flowers twice, in mid-winter and at Easter, coinciding with Christ's birth and death. Rather more prosaically, it has been identified as *Crategus monogyna* 'Biflora' as this cultivar flowers twice a year at those times.

The tree has been used in herbal medicine since ancient times but there are confusions, depending what you believe. Ancient beliefs held that blossom picked on Maundy Thursday would protect the house from lightning, a globe of woven hawthorn brought into the house would ensure that fairies protected the property from fire and that a branch hung over the front door would prevent evil spirits entering the house. However it is also widely believed that a branch brought into the house would cause a death in the family. This is possibly because hawthorn was regarded as the Virgin Mary's plant and in anti-Catholic times having a branch in the house would have indicated Catholic beliefs and might have endangered the family.

Lone trees in Ireland belong to fairies and should not be misused, even hanging washing on the branches could disturb unseen fairy laundry already hanging there. William Allingham makes the risks clear in his poem:

By the craggy hill-side,
Through the mosses bare,
They have planted thorn-trees
For pleasure here and there.
Is any man so daring
As dig them up in spite,

He shall find their sharpest thorns
In his bed at night.

(From *The Fairies*)

However according to a traditional nursery rhyme, dew on hawthorn bushes would give beauty to those who washed their faces in it on May Day:

The fair maid who the first of May
Goes to the field at the break of day
And washes in dew from the hawthorn tree
Will ever after handsome be.

(From *The First of May*)

We cynically note that the maid had to be fair in the first place.

HUCKLEBERRIES

The name may be a corruption of hurtleberry (blueberry) as the plants and fruits appear similar. Often the only way to tell the berries apart is to eat them and wait for the distinctive crunch of the huckleberry's larger seeds. Possibly because of these seeds, huckleberries are more commonly regarded as ornamental garden plants, rather than crops, although Native Americans used them to thicken and flavour game stews.

In America huckleberry was nineteenth-century slang used to describe unimportant people, the word becoming immortalized in Mark Twain's novel *Huckleberry Finn*. He may have used the name because he saw children collecting the berries on the way to deliver the manuscript of his earlier book, *The Innocents Abroad*, which was to become his first successful novel.

Henry David Thoreau describes a supper of huckleberries and

blueberries and was adamant that the berries should be foraged, rather than bought:

> The fruits do not yield their true flavour to the purchaser of them, nor to him who raises them for the market. There is but one way to obtain it, yet few take that way. If you would know the flavour of huckleberries, ask the cow-boy or the partridge. It is a vulgar error to suppose that you have tasted huckleberries who have never plucked them. A huckleberry never reaches Boston; they have not been known there since they grew on her three hills. The ambrosial and essential part of the fruit is lost with the bloom which is rubbed off in the market-cart, and they become mere provender.

(From *Walden*)

JAPANESE WINEBERRIES

These beautiful berries originally grew wild in China and Japan and were introduced to the West in the early twentieth century. Their Latin name, *Rubus phoenicolasius* describes the colour of the hairs or little prickles on the stems, *phoeniceus* meaning purple-red. This, in turn comes from Phoenicea where the cities of Tyre and Sidon produced the ancient Tyrian purple dye from the secretion of a sea-snail.

JUNEBERRIES

This common name arises because in temperate climates the fruit ripens in June and is used to describe many species of *Amelanchier*. The serviceberry (*Amelanchier laevis*) is so called because it flowers in mid spring and indicates that the ground has warmed up sufficiently to dig graves and hold services for those who had died during winter. Another *amelanchier*, the shadbush (*A. canadensis*) flowers at the same time as the shad, a choice fish, ('Waiter bring me shad roe' sang Ertha Kitt), makes its spring run in rivers.

JUNIPER

This is another tree with mixed associations. Hung above doors and windows on May Eve, juniper branches would keep away witches and the smoke from burning wood was reputed to deter demons and offer protection against the plague. However, dreaming of the tree was considered bad luck, although dreaming of the berries was felt to be lucky.

Native Americans dried the berries and baked them into cakes to eat during the lean winter months and in northern Europe dried, spiced juniper has always been an essential ingredient in sauerkraut. Originally most juniper berries grown in Britain were used as the flavouring for gin but now most berries for this are imported from Eastern Europe. Before, and after, the advent of barbed wire the prickly branches were often placed on top of stone walls as a deterrent to both man and animals.

The oil in the berries is an abortifacient, leading to the Victorian use of a hot bath and gin to get rid of unwanted babies, and the plant's common name of bastard killer. Right up until the 1990s it was possible to buy juniper pills for this purpose.

In Roman times, according to *The Greek Herbal of Dioscorides* juniper juice was mixed with oil to treat the following: 'It doth kill wormes that are in the ears and doth quiet their noise and hissings'. Not a nice thought.

MULBERRIES

Mulberries originated in Central Asia, spread to Europe along the ancient trade routes and thence to America. Their cultivation in Britain reached a peak in the sixteenth and seventeenth centuries but they were probably originally brought here by the Romans.

Mulberries are often called wise fruits because they only come into bud after any danger of frost has passed. Their Latin name *Morus* comes from the word *mora* meaning delay. John Evelyn recommended waiting until mulberry leaves appeared to 'bring your oranges etc boldly out of the conservatory'.

Black mulberries are the best fruit but, according to the tale of Pyramus and Thisbe in Ovid's *Metamorphoses*, these fruits were originally white. The two young lovers decided to elope, arranging to meet beneath a mulberry tree. Thisbe arrived first but was frightened by the roar of a lion and ran away, dropping her cloak. The lion, bloodstained from a recent kill, mauled the cloak and then left. Pyramus arrived, was devastated at the death of his love and stabbed himself to death. His blood stained the tree's roots and the berries turned from white to black. Sadly the tale ends with Thisbe returning to find her lover dying and killing herself as well. A warning against precipitate suicide which Romeo would have done well to heed.

The fruits of the white mulberry do turn red as they ripen but never develop the same depth of colour or flavour; this is the tree to grow for silk. Discovered in China in 2500 BC the manufacture of silk was a closely guarded secret with a death penalty for anyone caught smuggling silkworm eggs or mulberry seeds out of the country. Myths were also spread, such as that which said that the silkworm made its silken cocoon in the eyebrows of a beautiful maiden. By 3-400 AD the knowledge of how to make silk had spread to India and Japan, but it remained ruinously expensive in Europe, selling at its equivalent weight in gold in 526 AD. In the seventeenth century, James I decided to break this monopoly. He encouraged the planting of mulberry trees the length and breadth of the country but unfortunately all the trees produced black mulberries. Although it is possible to make silk from black mulberries, the white produce the finest silk as the leaves, which the worms eat, appear earlier and are more nutritious. The plan largely failed and many of the plantations became pleasure gardens. The scheme was slightly more successful in America where colonists were given a book on sericulture and required to plant trees, but here the production was eventually overtaken by cotton. Red mulberries thrive in America to this day even though little silk is made.

Mulberries are long-lived and many of those planted in James's reign survive today. Sadly the tree Shakespeare planted at Stratford-upon-Avon is not one of them. In 1752 Rev Francis Gastrell who owned the house cut the tree down as he was bored with showing it to visitors.

Mulberry trees are known to most children, by name if not by looks, from the rhyme *Here we go round the mulberry bush*. The rhyme describes a number of everyday activities and was one of many similar songs popular throughout Europe in the nineteenth and twentieth centuries. It may be a traditional song but the women's prison at Wakefield claims it as theirs. There was, and still is, a mulberry tree in the prison yard and their claim is that the women prisoners sang to entertain their children as they exercised round the tree.

Pliny the Elder describes a mouthwash which could be made from the berries saying, 'There is no other remedy more pleasant for the mouth, the trachea, the uvula or the gullet' (*Natural History*). The Romans also used them as hair dye, soaking the berries in a mixture of black fig leaves, wine and rainwater. In medieval times, tonsillitis was treated by taking mulberries soaked in honey.

MYRTLE

In Greek legend Myrrha was one of Venus' priestesses. When she was pursued by an unwanted suitor, for safety, she was transformed into a tree, the myrtle. In her memory the flowers were used in purification ceremonies and made into bridal wreaths.

In Romulus' temple in Rome there were two sacred myrtles: one representing the patricians, the other the plebeians. The fortunes of the two groups of citizens was said to be dictated by the respective trees.

Traditionally the berries were used to sweeten the breath and, like so many other dark berries, as hair dye.

RASPBERRIES

The Latin *idaeus* comes from Pliny the Elder's description of the wild fruit growing on Mount Ida in Crete. In Greek mythology, all raspberries were originally white. One day when baby Zeus was crying, the nymph Ida plucked some raspberries to quieten him. A thorn pricked her finger, her blood stained the berries red and they were named in her memory.

Hindberry is an old common name from the hinds or deer that ate the fruits. *Raspis*, a later name, possibly stems from the French red wine *respyce* or *raspis* which the juice of the berries resembled. It may equally come from the rough, rasping surface of the berries compared with the smoothness of blackberries.

Raspberries were gathered wild for thousands of years before they were cultivated; Native Americans often dried the wild berries so they could be carried more easily or stored for use in winter. In medieval times, the juice was used in paintings and illuminated manuscripts and historically in Britain they were commonly used as a medicine, particularly for sore eyes and stomach complaints. Mrs Beeton has the following recommendation: 'the berry itself is exceedingly wholesome, and invaluable to people of a nervous or bilious temperament'.

They became popular in the kitchen too and John Nott's *Cooks and Confectioners Dictionary* of 1726 had several recipes, including this for raspberry cakes:

> Take raspberries that are pretty ripe, and as much as they weigh in double-refin'd sugar, boil'd to a candy Height, with a little Water, having first bruis'd your Raspberries; put them into the Candy, and mingle them with it; then pot them into little Tin Hoops, or drop them on Plates; set them in a

Stove, and keep turning till they are dry. If you would have the Cakes without Seeds, you may strain your Raspberries.

Anyone wanting advice on jam-making need look no further than Tolstoy's novel *Anna Karenina*:

> That afternoon jam was being made on the terrace by a method new to Agafea Mihalovna, without the addition of water. Kitty had introduced this new method, which had been used in her home. Agafea Mihalovna, to whom the task of jam-making had always been entrusted, considering that what had been done in the Levin household could not be amiss, had nevertheless put water with the strawberries, maintaining that jam could not be made without it. She had been caught in the act, and it was to be proved to her conclusively that jam could be made very well without water.
>
> Agafea Mihalovna, her face heated and angry, her hair untidy, and her thin arms bare to the elbows, was turning the preserving-pan over the charcoal stove, looking darkly at the raspberries and devoutly hoping they would stick and not cook properly. The princess, conscious that Agafea Mihalovna's wrath must be chiefly directed against her, as the person responsible for the raspberry jam-making, tried to appear to be absorbed in other things and not interested in the jam, talked of other matters, but cast stealthy glances in the direction of the stove.

We are inclined to agree with Agafea.

ROWAN

Once planted as protection against witches, these trees are now commonly planted in cities because of their tolerance of pollution although clearly keeping the urban witch population in check is an added bonus. Traditionally, on May Eve, crosses were made without using a knife and tied with red thread to protect cattle from witches. Branches brought into the house on Good Friday would provide the same protection. Trees were planted in graveyards to stop the dead from rising and the wood was used for coffins and biers for the same reason. The branches were used for archer's bows, walking sticks and cream stirrers, presumably for supernatural protection as much as suppleness or strength.

Wild service trees, chequers and rowans are all closely related, belonging to the Sorbus genus. After the first winter frost, the fruits are bletted and can be eaten, although they were more commonly recommended for their medicinal 'binding' quality rather than their taste.

SEA BUCKTHORN

Sea buckthorn may today be known for tart, vitamin-filled berries, thorns, and an ability to grow on sand dunes but, according to John Lewis-Stempel's excellent and inspiring book on foraging, they were the favourite food of Pegasus. Most plant dictionaries link the Latin name (*Hippophae rhamnoides*) to the Greek *rhamnos* meaning thorny shrub, but we prefer his explanation that the name stems from the Greek for 'glittering horse' and that the leaves were fed to race horses.

STRAWBERRIES

The name possibly comes from the Anglo-Saxon *streow berrie* or *streabariye*, meaning a berry which strays, alluding to the runners the plants put out. It may also come from the old practice of threading wild berries onto straws of grass to take to the local market to sell. It is unlikely that it refers to the straw that was traditionally spread round the plants to protect the berries from damp soil as the name was common long before the fruits were cultivated. The Latin name

Fragaria clearly refers to the fruit's fragrance, a sharp reminder that fragrantless and flavourless berries should be avoided.

Wild strawberries only grew wild in Europe north of the Alps, so they were unknown to the Ancient Greeks, but from as far back as 200 BC there are records of Romans trying to domesticate wild strawberries and grow larger fruits. In the Middle Ages they were grown for ornamental and medicinal purposes, with the fruit being recommended both as toothpaste and to ease sunburn. However, Gerard says scathingly in his *Herball*: 'The nourishment which they yield is little, thin and waterish, and if they happen to putrify in the stomach, their nourishment is naught'.

Whatever their medicinal value, strawberries have long been regarded as aphrodisiacs; a soup of strawberries, soured cream and borage was traditionally an important part of wedding breakfasts. The first record of strawberries and cream is at an English banquet in 1509 and they have remained popular ever since, immortalized in the Mother Goose nursery rhyme:

Curly locks, curly locks wilt thou be mine?
Thou shall't not wash dishes, nor yet feed the swine,
But sit on a cushion and sew a fine seam,
And feed upon strawberries, sugar and cream.

By the seventeenth century, wild strawberries were recognized as a delicacy, prompting the physician William Butler to say 'Doubtless God could have made a better berry, but doubtless God never did'. John Nott's *Cooks and Confectioners Dictionary* of 1726 recommends 'strawberries are usually eaten soaked in Water and Wine, and strew'd with Sugar; but they may be iced and preserved as well dry as liquid'.

John Tradescant, the Elder gardener to, amongst others, King James I, discovered an unusual strawberry in 1628, which is still available today. He rescued the plant from a garden in Plymouth where, 'finding the fruit not to answer her expectation', the owner was about to throw it away. A strange plant, it has green flowers and fruits like spiky hedgehogs. For many years it was thought to have died out but it then turned up in the garden of the Gloucestershire clergyman Canon Ellacombe. He passed it on to the gardener and writer E.A. Bowles who planted it in his garden at Myddleton House, Enfield in an area he described as a 'lunatic asylum' devoted to botanical misfits and curiosities. Today it is know as the Plymouth strawberry or 'Muricata'.

The wild strawberries which grew in England produced delicious fruits, but they were small and cropped erratically. The hunt was still on for a plant which produced large tasty fruits and cropped reliably. The hautbois, hautboys or alpine strawberries of Europe were larger, but the two could not be crossed. The aim of gardeners was to have a fruit which was larger than the British wild strawberry, which cropped regularly, but retained the flavour. In the seventeenth century the Virginian strawberry (*Fragaria virginiana*) was brought to Europe. The Native Americans had eaten these berries and mixed them with Indian corn meal to make bread and the early settlers wrote home extolling the berries' virtues. They flowered and fruited in Europe, but not spectacularly and still did not give the gardeners the large fruits they craved. In 1712 a large, pale, yellowy-red strawberry (*F. chiloensis*) was brought to France from South America by a French naval officer, Captain A. F. Frézier. This became popular throughout Europe, but mostly as a curiosity as it had little flavour. The French botanist Duchesne realized that the two American strawberries could be crossed, but research in France was hindered by the upheavals of the Revolution. The English took over the experimentation and in 1821 Michael Keen produced 'Keen's Seedling' at his market garden in Isleworth, a plant with fruits that were both large and well-flavoured. This was the first of most of our modern strawberries and earned Keen a Silver Cup from the Royal Horticultural Society.

William Morris's famous pattern *The Strawberry Thief* was inspired when he saw a thrush eating strawberries in his garden at Kelmscott Manor. The strawberry patch still exists in the garden and one would like to think that descendants of the same bird are stealing the fruit.

In Grimm's fairy tale a beautiful and sweet-tempered girl is sent out by her wicked stepmother to look for strawberries in the snow.

The girl makes the point that strawberries don't grow in winter but this is the land of fairy tales and, after helping three little men, she of course finds plenty of delicious ripe berries. In case you're wondering, the girl ends up married to a kind king and the stepmother gets her comeuppance.

Out-of-season berries have always been a treat and in Thomas Hardy's *Tess of the d'Urbevilles* Alec Stoke d'Urbeville uses them to seduce Tess as he shows her round the garden:

> Tess wished to abridge her visit as much as possible; but the young man was pressing and she assented to accompany him. He conducted her about the lawns, and the flower-beds, and the conservatories; and thence to the fruit-garden and the greenhouses, where he asked if she liked strawberries. 'Yes,' said Tess, 'when they come.' 'They are already here.' D'Urberville began gathering specimens of the fruit for her, handing them back to her as he stooped; and, presently, selecting a specially fine product of the 'British Queen' variety, he stood up and held it by the stem to her mouth. 'No – no!' she said quickly, putting her fingers between his hand and her lips. 'I would rather take it in my own hand.' 'Nonsense!' he insisted; and in a slight distress she parted her lips and took it in.

The perfect luxury with which to seduce a country girl.

BERRIES FOR HEALTH

Eat Food. Not too much. Mainly plants.

(Michael Pollan *In Defence of Food*)

These words from food activist Michael Pollan provide an excellent mantra for those in search of a healthy lifestyle. Food in its natural state is far more delicious and far, far better for you than any array of dietary supplements. Preparing your own meals doesn't have to be difficult and can be a relaxing counterpoint to the stress of a busy day. As the great Elizabeth David noted, an omelette and a glass of wine is the perfect supper and throwing together a salad can be quicker than getting a takeaway. The ideal, of course, is preparing your own meals from ingredients you have grown yourself. That way you know exactly what you are eating and have total control over what you are putting in your body. If you can't grow your own, then consider buying organic or from a local pick-your-own or farmers market where you can ask about varieties and the pesticides and herbicides used on the produce. Of course we all have busy days and lazy days, and days when all you want to put in your body is a bar of chocolate but make that one bar and a good quality chocolate and you can't go too far wrong. As our mothers always said 'A little of what you fancy does you good'.

In the history section (page 11 onwards) you will read about some of the ancient folk remedies using berries employed by our ancestors. As with all old wives' tales there is a mixture of common sense, nutritional science and just plain tosh in many of these. Today's consumer adopts a more scientific approach to health and there has been much research on the make-up of foods which helps explain why berries are so good for us. Please bear in mind that although health claims may be based on analysis of the nutritional content of the berries in many cases they have not been officially tested or approved by the medical community.

We firmly believe that the best reason to eat berries is because they taste amazing but when you look into it they are also tremendously good for you. If you make berries part of your regular diet, and there are different berries available year round so you can, then you will be taking a big step toward the healthy lifestyle you deserve.

Berries taste great eaten fresh from the garden and this is usually the healthiest and the easiest way to consume them. Frozen berries are also a good choice as flash-frozen they retain all of their vitamins and nutrients. Naturally-dried berries, those you have dehydrated yourself, are just berries with the water taken out and are nearly as good as fresh although some of the vitamins, notably C, B and A are slightly reduced by the dehydration process.

The British Dietetic Association advocates berries as low in calories and high in nutrients and a perfect choice as one of your five a day. The recipes we have given you on pages 109-205 will show you how to incorporate more berries in your diet. Here are some of the reasons why you should eat more berries.

ANTIOXIDANTS

Perhaps the most overwhelming factor in favour of berries, is that they are one of the best and tastiest sources of antioxidants available to us. An antioxidant is a molecule that inhibits the oxidization of other molecules. The most common antioxidants are vitamins A, C and E, beta carotene, selenium and lycopene.

The very processes of living: breathing, creating and using energy, produce free radicals in our bodies. Free radicals are single atoms, which have too many or too few electrons making them unstable. In order to stabilize themselves, they dump their excess electrons or take new ones from other molecules, in turn upsetting their balance; this chain reaction causes cell damage, which in turn leads to ageing and predisposes us to cancer and other illnesses. Put simply, just existing is bad for us.

Other factors of modern life such as stress, pollution, pesticides, smoking, drinking and sunlight exacerbate the situation. Increasing the levels of antioxidants in our diet can help to neutralize the free radicals and stop them causing damage. Antioxidants do this by halting or slowing the chain reaction leading to oxidization or by becoming oxidized themselves, in effect taking the hit for you. Think of that strawberry as a little fruit in a lycra jumpsuit leaping in front of the bullet whizzing towards you. Now eat him, ideally with cream.

Water-soluble pigments called anthocyanins are one of the most important groups of phytochemicals acting as antioxidants. These are found in high quantities in most berries. They are in the pigments that give berries their colour and as a rule of thumb the darker the colour of the berry the higher the level of anthocyanins. They act as an antivirus solution helping to protect against disease before it starts.

Tannins occur in high concentrations in many berries, particularly cranberries, and they are a form of antioxidant known as polyphenols. They act as barriers to infection particularly in the mouth and urinary tract.

Vitamins

Vitamins are an important component of a healthy diet. Different vitamins have different roles to play and often only small amounts (as little as a few milligrams) are necessary. Some such as A,D,E and K can be stored in the body but others such as C and B are water soluble and amounts in excess of our daily needs are excreted away so we need to ensure that they are consumed on an ongoing and regular basis. Some of the key vitamins in berries include are:

Vitamin A (retinal) which is beneficial in eye and skin health and for growth. The body can convert beta-carotene, an important antioxidant in its own right, into retinal.

Vitamin B. There are six water-soluble vitamins in the B group and they work together to promote the growth and development of a healthy nervous system, for body maintenance and to support the metabolism. They need to be consumed regularly as they cannot be stored in the body.

Vitamin C is probably the most well-known of the vitamins, traditionally taken to reduce and mitigate against the effects of colds and flu. It plays a key protective role in maintaining the immune system and is necessary for building healthy bones and teeth and in the healing process. It also assists the absorption of iron. Low levels of vitamin C are associated with high blood pressure and the increased risk of heart attack. There is some suggestion that vitamin C can dilute the arteries and assist in improved blood flow. New research suggests it may also reduce the risk of osteoarthritis.

Vitamin E works to increase the body's immune response and to protect against diseases including cancer. It is also important for maintaining healthy skin and healing damaged tissue and in slowing down cellular aging due to oxidation.

Vitamin K is important for the normal clotting of blood and to help wounds heal. It also assists in the maintenance of healthy bones.

MINERALS AND TRACE ELEMENTS

Berries provide a hefty dose of some of the minerals needed for a healthy life. In general the three main functions of minerals are: as constituents of bones and teeth (particularly calcium, magnesium and phosphorus), as salts regulating body fluids (sodium, potassium and chloride) and as components of enzymes and hormones.

Trace elements like manganese activate enzymes which are essential for the body's use of B1 and C vitamins and for the effective operation of the thyroid. Manganese helps to maintain memory function, prevent osteoporosis and aids proper muscle reflexes. Copper, another trace element found in some berries, cannot be manufactured by the body and so must be ingested. It is essential to the proper development of bones and organs and in the formation of red blood cells. It further stimulates the immune system to fight infection and to promote healing.

Fat and Fibre

Berries are in themselves low in calories. Clearly you can change that if you only ever eat them with cream or in butter-rich baking but you are starting with a very healthy low-fat ingredient. If you are eating dried berries remember the dehydration process concentrates the energy and calorie value in a smaller portion size. This is an advantage if you are hiking but less so if you are on a diet. Another thing to watch for if you are buying commercially dried berries is that sugar may have been added during processing; just be careful to check the label.

Remember berries are also surprisingly high in fibre, raspberries in particular. A cup of raspberries provides nearly 30% of a woman's daily fibre requirements. Fibre as well as aiding in digestive health ensures you feel fuller and eat less.

Bone and Joint Health

The Arthritis Foundation encourages the eating of berries to ease the pain and other symptoms of rheumatoid arthritis. The anthocyanin found in red and purple berries has an anti-inflammatory effect. The Foundation recommends incorporating three different berries into your daily diet. Foods high in fibre, as berries are, are also said to reduce the amount of C-reactive protein, a marker that indicates the level of inflammation in the body. The high levels of vitamin C are a further advantage as vitamin C assists with collagen production laying down cartilage stores which help with joint flexibility.

In addition to these general benefits to boosting your berry intake there are some specific benefits associated with particular berries which we have outlined below.

ACAI BERRIES

Currently hailed as botox in a berry, this Brazilian berry is most commonly available in juice or supplement form as it deteriorates quickly after harvest. Acai is particularly high in antioxidants (twice the level of blueberries) and contains omega three fatty acids, amino acids, fibre and iron. In its native habitat of the Amazon rain forest it has traditionally been combined with guarana seeds to make tonics claiming to provide energy and improve mental clarity.

BILBERRIES

Bilberries or blueberries are associated with eye health and in particular the improvement of night vision. There are stories, probably apocryphal, about RAF pilots consuming bilberry jam in preparation for night missions.

BLACKBERRIES

Along with raspberries and strawberries, blackberries are high in ellagic acid. This is believed to help protect against sun damage and to inhibit the growth of melanomas. A dark coloured berry, they are high in antioxidants and contain good levels of vitamins A, E and K, potassium, manganese and copper. The bark and leaves of blackberries used to be pounded down to make a treatment for dysentery.

BLUEBERRIES

Blueberries are one of the few berries that have claims based on medical trials. The Nurses' Health Study which has been ongoing since the 1970s reported a 32% lower risk of heart attacks amongst women eating three or more portions of blueberries and strawberries a week although the study was unable to prove definitively that blueberry consumption was the sole cause. However blueberries are extremely high in antioxidants, low in calories and high in fibre. They also are also a good source of vitamin K and C and manganese.

CRANBERRIES

The consumption of cranberries and cranberry juice has long been advocated for those suffering from recurrent urinary tract infections, as it seems to provide some relief particularly against cystitis. They are a natural probiotic supporting the growth of healthy bacteria in the gastrointestinal tract and aiding digestion.

It has been reported that there is a compound in cranberries which helps to block the enzymes that form plaque and lead to tooth decay although a lot of cranberry products (notably cranberry juice) contain added sugars and large scale consumption can of course lead to tooth decay. As always read the label on any processed product and watch out for added sugar content.

ELDERBERRIES

Elderberries are very high in Vitamin C and are traditionally used in cold and flu remedies and to boost the immune system. Caution needs to be employed in the use and consumption of elderberries as the green parts of the plant are poisonous and the berries mildly toxic until cooked which removes the low levels of cyanide.

Goji Berries

These have been used in Chinese medicine for centuries. There is a great deal of hype around the goji berry at the moment hailing it as the fruit of Shangri-La, an anti-aging miracle. In fact the high levels of antioxidants do mean they are good for you. There are unproven claims that the consumption of goji berries can boost the immune system and brain activity, protect against heart disease and cancer and improve life expectancy. As with so many berries the claims are based on the content of vitamins C, B2, A, iron, selenium and other antioxidants in which these berries are rich. Because they bruise so easily, goji berries are most often available dried and are usually soaked before adding to a dish. Soaking the berries has the advantage of ensuring a thorough wash, which will remove any dust or impurities which may have attached themselves to your healthful berries before they reach you.

Juniper

The most common association with juniper is gin and the British Empire is founded on the efforts of those who swore by a stiff G&T as an essential bastion against malaria. Of course we now know the quinine was in the tonic rather than the gin. Juniper has been widely used in medicines for centuries. It is a natural antibacterial and is often used in topical applications to treat wounds or to calm skin conditions including eczema, warts and athlete's foot. Taken internally it reduces stomach acids and inflammation and is considered to have anti-flatulent properties. It also stimulates the kidneys and acts as a diuretic. It is recommended that juniper be avoided by pregnant women as it can be used to stimulate menstruation and to bring on labour.

Mulberries

Mulberries have been used for centuries to treat sore throats. Unusually among berries, mulberries are a good source of iron containing 1.85 mg per 100 g which is nearly a quarter of the recommended daily allowance. Traditional European folk medicine used mulberries as a treatment for tapeworm. If you eat enough mulberries they have laxative properties but then again most fruit, particularly if unripe, can have this effect if you eat enough of it. A fact often demonstrated by overly greedy children let loose in the orchard.

Raspberries

Raspberries are extremely high in fibre and water and thus are helpful in maintaining digestive health. One cup of raspberries can provide just over half of your daily vitamin needs being high in vitamins K and E, folate, iron, copper, potassium and flavonoids for heart health. Traditionally raspberries and more particularly raspberry leaf tea have had a key role in women's health. Consumption of raspberry leaf tea is thought to aid in the reduction of menstrual flow and cramps and to lessen the pain of childbirth. It is also given to lactating mothers to increase milk flow.

Sea Buckthorn

Sea buckthorn berries have a strong red colour and are particularly high in carotene. Their vitamin C content is amongst the highest of any fruit. They also contain palmeotolic acid which is alleged to have benefits in promoting the elasticity of the skin and even in skin cell regeneration. For this reason extract of sea buckthorn is often used in skin creams. The oil has also been used in the treatment of burns and was used on the survivors of Chernobyl to help with radiation burns.

Sloes

Sloes are an astringent berry which stimulates the metabolism, cleanses the blood and can be used as a diuretic. Historically, sloes were brewed as a purgative to treat fluxes of the belly.

STRAWBERRIES

Strawberries are excellent sources of vitamins C and K, fibre, folic acid, manganese and potassium. Micronutrients present in strawberries include quercetin which some research has suggested can protect against heart disease and strokes.

Historically they have been used to help with digestive ailments and to alleviate skin irritations. That said, allergy to strawberries is a common, albeit clearly unfortunate, allergy which often manifests itself in a rash.

Interestingly pairing strawberries with high cacao content chocolate (88% and above) is said to boost the nutritive value of both products - an excellent argument in favour of chocolate-dipped strawberries.

Strawberries are high in folic acid which has been shown to play a role in combatting birth defects in pregnant women. It has also been suggested that folic acid deficiency can be a contributing factor in dementia, heart disease and osteoporosis.

BERRIES IN THE HEDGEROW

The value of these fruits is not in the mere possession or eating of them, but in the sight and enjoyment of them.

(Henry David Thoreau, *Wild Fruits*)

This section is not intended as a foraging guide, more an encouragement to go out and collect berries and have fun. You don't have to go miles to an isolated spot in the country to forage; parks, city streets, public gardens and paths can all yield a surprising amount of delicious free food. There is a fine line between wild and cultivated fruits; most of the plants in cities will have been carefully cultivated, but it is often possible to pick from them just as you would a plant in the wild.

One of the joys of foraging is that you can have all the benefits of home-grown fruit with none of the work. Nature and the seasons do all the gardening for you. We have been farmers for 10,000 years, but foragers or hunter-gatherers for over 200,000. There are over 400 food plants growing in Britain alone. This doesn't mean that they are all appetizing, that you are likely to find them, or indeed that you should pick them, as some are now rare. Here we have mentioned berries that you are likely to be able to find, even if some live in specialized places, and which are worth eating, although some could be described as interesting, rather than delicious.

Look on foraging as a joyous bonus to your cooking, rather than a means of survival. John Lewis-Stempel proved that it was perfectly possible to survive by foraging for a year (*Wild Life*), but, fascinating and inspiring as the book was, his diet was repetitive and he at times ate things which managed to sound both dull and disgusting.

At the risk of sounding like bossy teachers, we would like to point out that to forage happily and safely, there are various rules you should follow.

Most importantly, you must make sure you know exactly what you are eating. Ideally use more than one guide book so you can compare and contrast, or go on a tour guided by an expert. Don't jump to conclusions and never eat anything because it looks *roughly* like something (pictures on the internet are notoriously misleading and are even, on occasion, wrongly labelled). The identification of berries is much less hazardous than mushrooms, but there are berries that can kill you. Some berries, such as mahonia, berberis and hawthorn, are best eaten in moderation; others, such as brambles and mulberries you can safely eat to your heart's content. There is a list of the most poisonous berries to be aware of on page 57. Some people may suffer allergic reactions to otherwise harmless plants so always take care when trying something for the first time.

Foraging laws vary hugely. In Scotland there are statutory access rights and you can walk almost anywhere, foraging as you go, as long as you don't damage the property in any way, although remember that picking fruit could, by some, be described as damaging. In America, laws of trespass are strict and foraging is often forbidden. Elsewhere in Britain and in Europe there is a minefield of bye-laws, rules and sub-clauses; in some places you can walk but not forage, in others you can forage, but only for your own domestic use. The best guidelines are to get permission whenever you can and use your common sense. There is a huge difference between picking blackberries for a pie and collecting baskets of them to make jam commercially.

Avoid busy roads, both for safety and fumes; the other side of the hedge would be less polluted and more pleasant. Check agricultural land hasn't been sprayed with chemicals and that industrial sites aren't polluted. In areas where animals may have passed by, always pick above waist height, and in any case this makes picking easier.

If you are collecting berries in an urban park, you are unlikely to come across anything more dangerous than a wasp, but in the countryside there can be anything from snakes to bears, depending on which country's countryside you are in. It may not be applicable for a British park, but there is an old Indian saying 'Look first for the berries, and then the bear, when bear hunting'. Take any necessary precautions before you go and be aware that these animals consider the countryside theirs as much as you do.

Respect other foragers; many birds and wild animals eat berries, but while we pick largely for pleasure, they depend on these foods for survival. Always leave enough on the plant for the next forager.

Also respect the plant. For many plants, berries are their seeds, the means by which they will grow new plants. Pick gently and be careful not to damage shoots and stems and don't trample thoughtlessly through the land. Never dig up a plant growing in the wild, even if it seems abundant. By using the countryside sensibly, foragers are actually protecting it. Picking berries rarely endangers plants; loss of their natural habitats to agriculture or building is far more threatening.

You can use anything you like to collect your berries. Baskets look charming, but are cumbersome; plastic bags tend to squash the fruit and nearly always develop a leak at some crucial point. Plastic ice-cream cartons are not things of beauty, but they are invaluable as they protect the fruit and once they are full you can put the lid on. We also use the containers you are given at some pick-your-own farms; sturdy card baskets with plastic liners.

Two points that guide books rarely mention are the dyeing propensity of many berries and the risk of backache. In our experience purple or dark red clothes are more important than protective kit. A few scratches rarely do any long term harm and if you are wearing clothes that are already a suitable colour you won't need to worry about juice stains. Many berries grow on inconveniently low bushes.

When harvesting, take time to stretch out, lie on your back in the sunshine and perhaps enjoy some of your crop. Remember, foraging should be fun.

THE FORAGING YEAR

This is a rough guide to harvesting times. However, a June day in the Cairngorms of Scotland can be very different to the same day on the South Downs of England and local conditions will also affect ripening. You will soon learn when your local berries are at their best.

Early summer: elderflowers, gooseberries, wild strawberries

Mid summer: elderflowers, gooseberries, mulberries, wild raspberries, sea buckthorn, wild strawberries

Late summer: bilberries, brambles, cloudberries, cranberries, elderberries, juniper berries, mahonia, mulberries, wild raspberries, rowan berries, sea buckthorn, wild strawberries

Early autumn: bilberries, brambles, elderberries, hawthorn berries, juniper berries, lingonberries, mahonia, rowan berries, sea buckthorn, sloes, wild strawberries

Mid autumn: brambles, cranberries, hawthorn berries, juniper berries, lingonberries, rowan berries, sea buckthorn, sloes

Late autumn: juniper berries, rowan berries, sea buckthorn, sloes

Early winter: rowan berries, sloes

THE BERRIES

Below is a small selection of some of the best berries to forage. Many have escaped from gardens and naturalized themselves and, equally, many wild fruits are now commonly grown in gardens. Use the list of ornamental garden plants on pages 104-108 too.

Bilberries and Wild Blueberries (*Vaccinium* spp.)

Bilberry, blaeberry, cowberry, fraughan, heatherberry, hurts, myrtille, sparkleberry, whinberry, whortleberry and wimberry are all the same fruit, the different names depending on where you live. Bilberries grow on low spreading shrubs which need acid soil and are mostly found on windswept heaths and moors. They are backbreaking to collect as the plants are low and you need to look below the leaves to find the berries. A special coarse-toothed, wooden and metal comb called a bilberry comb or a *peignes à myrtilles* can make harvesting slightly easier, but you tend to collect a lot of twigs and leaves as well as the fruit. Even so, it is worth collecting bilberries, as their flavour is so much better than shop-bought blueberries. Wild blueberries have the advantage of growing on taller plants. They too often have a better flavour than cultivated fruits. Blueberry bushes can easily be found in city parks and gardens where the soil is naturally acidic and will give you the satisfaction of foraging without backache or a trip to the moors.

Bearberries (*Arctostaphylos uva-ursi*) and crowberries (*Empetrum nigrum*) look similar to bilberries, but tend to be a bit watery and tasteless. Their common names may come from the fact that bears and crows eat the berries, or from the fact that they are only fit for bears and crows. Apparently they taste better cooked, but we prefer to reserve our energies for bilberries. All these berries can be used in any blueberry or cranberry recipe.

Blackberries and Brambles (*Rubus* spp.)

Bramble picking heralds the beginning of the end of summer. It is possible to get sun burned picking them, but the evenings will be cool enough for a substantial pudding such as Blackberry and Apple Pie (page 133) or the Bramble Steamed Puddings on page 129. The berries are easy to find; they will quickly colonize any neglected patch of ground, are often planted in old hedgerows and were traditionally planted round churchyards to keep sheep out. Brambles interbreed merrily and there are hundreds of micro-species in Britain and probably thousands worldwide, but they all look roughly the same and are all edible; you just may find some are sweeter or juicier than others. The berries at the tip of each stem ripen first and are supposedly the tastiest. The berries are delicate so pick from an area where you won't need to wash them, i.e. avoid roadsides and low branches where animals have been. The long arching stems have vicious thorns; you can either go armed in thick tweed, gloves and wellies or suffer a few scratches. Either way, wear old or purple clothes as they will get stained with juice.

When Lucifer was cast out of Paradise on Michaelmas Day, he supposedly landed in a blackberry bush. You shouldn't pick any berries after that day (29 September or 12 October, depending on whether you are using the modern Gregorian calendar or the old Julian one which is now thirteen days behind) as every year the devil returns to spit, stamp or do something more even unmentionable on them. There is sense in this, as by this time of year there are less hours of sunshine and an increased risk of frost, and the fruit will have less flavour. Any brambles can be substituted in blackberry or raspberry recipes.

Blackthorn or Sloes (*Prunus spinosa*)

Blackthorn is an apt name as the trees have a very dark wood, which looks particularly beautiful early in the year, with the pure white blossom. They also have vicious thorns, if the common name wasn't warning enough; their Latin name, *Prunus spinosa,* repeats the caution. The trees can be found in gardens or, more commonly, old hedgerows. The dark, dusty blue sloes appear in early autumn and can be picked up until the start of winter. They are too tart to eat raw but are delicious in jelly, cordial and, of course, as a liqueur with gin or vodka.

CLOUDBERRIES (*Rubus chamaemorus*)

These berries are also known as baked apple berries, knoutberries, nubs, salmonberries or yellow berries and are found in the boggy northern heath lands of Scotland, Scandinavia, Russia and Canada. They thrive in cold weather, growing well within the Arctic Circle. The golden orange berries ripen slowly, developing a rich, sweet flavour. Quite hard to find and backbreaking to pick, it is all worth it when you eat the fruit fresh with ice cream or make it into jam.

CRANBERRIES (*Vaccinium* spp.)

These berries are not particularly easy to find, even on the acidic bogs and heaths they favour. Much of their natural habitat has been drained for agriculture and, unlike brambles, they are fussy colonizers. Raw they are too sharp to eat, but a few added to apple or pear dishes or milky puddings and custards make a huge difference. Luckily, a little goes a long way in both sweet and savoury recipes.

ELDERBERRIES AND ELDERFLOWERS (*Sambucus nigra*)

Elderflowers have an honorary place in this book on berries as elderflower cordial is one of the joys of summer. Every year Jane goes foraging for the flower heads to a secret location in south-west London with her friend Louy. We aren't saying where, but we have provided Louy's recipe for cordial on page 202. The flowers form large, flat, creamy-coloured heads and should be treated gently. For the best flavour, pick on a dry, sunny day; rain washes away the pollen, which is where the flavour lies. Cut the stalks when the flowers are fully open, but avoid any that are brownish as they will be past their best. Don't wash them, but shake to dislodge any insects. They can also be made into an alcoholic 'champagne', face cream or dipped in batter and fried. Remember that the flowers later become the berries, so forage accordingly. Wordsworth's poem *Foresight* is about strawberries, but the extract below could just as easily be applied to elderflowers:

> God has given a kindlier power
> To the favoured strawberry-flower.
> Hither soon as spring is fled
> You and Charles and I will walk;
> Lurking berries, ripe and red,
> Then will hang on every stalk,
> Each within its leafy bower;
> And for that promise spare the flower!

The clusters of small berries turn black when fully ripe and the stems a distinctive pinky-red. The easiest way to collect the berries is to cut the clusters with scissors. Raw berries are mildly toxic, so don't be tempted to nibble while you harvest. These stems are poisonous so you should remove the berries; stripping them with a fork is the easiest way. You then have to pick out any unripe green berries or wrinkled, over-ripe ones. All this palaver is worthwhile though, for the delicious flavour once the berries are cooked and made into jelly, vinegar, wine or cordial.

GOOSEBERRIES (*Ribes* spp.)

Also known as goosegogs, these plants do grow wild in Britain, but those you find are more likely to be escapees from gardens where birds have dropped the seeds. The bushes are thorny, but the fruits grow at a reasonable height so although you will get juice and blood-stained fingers, you won't get backache. We foragers like to count our blessings.

Hawthorn (*Crategus* spp.)

This is also called azzy tree, bread and cheese tree (from the edible young leaves and buds in spring), fairy thorn, whitethorn or May. Hawthorn means hedge thorn and the small trees were widely planted in Britain in the eighteenth and nineteenth centuries, when much common land was enclosed for agriculture. Old hedges are still a good place to forage, both for haws and other berries. In the past foraging was a more common activity and Culpeper says: 'I do not mean to trouble my readers with the description of a tree so universally known to almost every inhabitant of this kingdom.' The fragrant white flowers of hawthorn are one of the first signs of summer and the red berries or haws which follow herald the start of autumn. They can be eaten raw or cooked, but are best as jelly.

Juniper (*Juniperus communis*)

You have to be careful with junipers as not all are edible; the one you want is the common juniper (*Juniperus communis*). These berries are actually cones; if you look closely you can see the overlapping layers. The green berries on female trees only ripen and turn black in their second or third year. The fruits on the male trees contain the pollen sacs and will remain greenish yellow and inedible. Picking is fiddly as the ripe berries grow alongside unripe ones and all are surrounded by sharp needles; this is a time when it is worth wearing gloves. Junipers are a protected species in the UK, so only pick the berries if there are a lot of bushes; you will only need a few berries anyway.

Juniper berries provide the chief flavour for gin. In many countries it is illegal to distil your own spirits and even though it is possible to make gin using other methods, we think it is better to buy gin and use the berries for other recipes. In particular, they give a wonderful spiciness to meat, game and all types of cabbage. Be aware that they contain various potentially harmful compounds, an abortifacient in particular, which earned them the name bastard killer in Victorian times. To be safe, do not give juniper to expectant or nursing mothers or anyone suffering from kidney problems.

Lingonberries (*Vaccinium vitis-idaea*)

Clusterberry, cowberry, crowberry and foxberry are just a few of the common names for these berries. They grow on low shrubs which thrive on acidic moors and woodlands, but can be hard to find now as their native habitats have been reduced by farming and building. The little red berries are not particularly nice raw, but will add sparkle to apple or cabbage dishes. They can also be made into a wonderful jam or jelly, which goes well with poultry, venison and salmon.

Mulberries (*Morus nigra*)

If you don't have room to grow a mulberry tree, you will need to forage for the berries as you can rarely buy them. Parks and gardens are a good place to look; you can tell when the berries are ripe as the ground round the tree will be stained purple. This is an occasion to wear your oldest and most purple clothes. The berries are so juicy that it is best to collect them in a watertight container, such as an old ice cream carton.

Wild Raspberries (*Rubus idaeus* and spp.)

Local names include framboise or hindberry. These berries often get ignored as they look like unripe brambles. The easy way to tell the two plants apart is that wild raspberries have pale green leaves and softer thorns. Pick gently, don't wash and use as you would cultivated fruits, assuming you don't eat them all on the way home.

Rowan, Wild Service and Chequer Berry (*Sorbus* spp.)

Rowans can be found in hedges, woodlands, parks, gardens and city streets and are also known as mountain ash, quickbeam or wickentree. The creamy-white blossom is followed by striking autumn colour and red, yellow, white or orange berries which can be picked right through to late autumn. The trees are easiest to identify by their leaves so it is best to earmark your trees before they lose their leaves and then pop back once the berries are ready to harvest. Similar berries are the sorb, wild service and chequer, which become sweet once bletted. Raw rowan berries are often poisonous, sour and really more pip than flesh, which is a shame as the trees are so abundant. Cooked they become safe and more palatable and can be made into a jelly with apples which complements lamb and all types of game.

Sea Buckthorn (*Hippophae rhamnoides*)

Sea buckthorn is also known as sallow thorn and the bushes are common in coastal areas, often right on the beach. They are distinctive with their grey-green leaves and bright orange berries. They are fiddly to pick as sharp thorns lurk between the leaves and the berries have an annoying tendency to burst. The juice is really all you need, so the easiest way is to simply squeeze the berries over a bowl. A deep pudding bowl works best. Then sieve the juice into a lidded container. Pick before the hard winter frosts as after this the berries start to lose their colour and flavour. They taste like sherbetty vitamin C tablets in a surprising and not unpleasant way. They are best made into cordials, jellies or syrup and they go particularly well with white chocolate. A version of the Blueberry White Chocolate Terrine on page 120 made with sea buckthorn would be delicious.

Wild Strawberries (*Fragaria vesca*)

Wild strawberries are smaller and more delicate then cultivated ones. These berries fall into the back-breaking category as the plants are low-growing and the fruits often hide beneath the leaves. Don't go out aiming for a large haul, but appreciate the little jewels as you find them.

POISONOUS BERRIES

Eating berries is not as risky as eating mushrooms, but you should bear in mind that some berries are very poisonous and others, such as elderberries and many rowans, need to be cooked to make them safe. Most harmful berries are easy to recognize but, if you aren't absolutely sure you've identified a berry correctly, don't eat it. The following berries are poisonous and should be strictly avoided:

Black bryony, (*Tamus communis*), deadly nightshade (*Atropa belladonna*), holly (*Ilex* spp.), ivy (*Hedera* spp.), lords and ladies (*Arum maculatum*), mistletoe (*Viscum album*), nightshade (*Solanum* spp.) (annual or garden huckleberries (*Solanum scabrum*) are an exception, but you are unlikely to find them growing wild), privet (*Ligustrum* spp.), snowberries or ghostberries (*Symphoricarpos albus*), so called as they are food for ghosts, Virginia creeper (*Parthenocissus* spp.) and yew (*Taxus baccata*).

BERRIES IN THE GARDEN

Nothing is better than a fruit in its own proper season, perfectly ripened and handled with care, by the people who harvest it.

(Alice Waters, *Chez Panisse Fruit*)

There are a great many advantages to growing your own berries, not least the pleasure of going into the garden and picking a perfectly ripe berry to eat then and there. It will have a freshness and flavour that you rarely find in shop-bought produce and you will know exactly how it has been grown. You can also grow less-common berries and experiment with different varieties. You don't necessarily need much space and many of the plants are extremely beautiful, as well as being productive.

Fruit tastes best if it is allowed to ripen on the plant but, for ease of transportation, commercially-grown fruit is nearly always picked when it is still firm and unripe. Anything you pick from your own garden is guaranteed to taste better. The berries you grow will also give your cooking a proper sense of the seasons; you will eagerly await the first gooseberry and then, as they start to peter out, you will have the pleasure of the first crop of raspberries.

Before you rush out and buy any plants, you should consider which plants you will be able to grow and which ones you would like to grow. There is no point trying to grow huge, sun-loving plants if you have a small, shady patio and equally, there is no point growing berries you do not want to eat, unless they are exceptionally beautiful. Climate, soil, aspect and shelter are all important considerations. You may be able to modify some of them, but you should take stock of what you have. Blackberries, for example, will grow in almost any soil, whereas blueberries have very specific requirements.

Most berries grow on perennial plants, shrubs or trees, which means that they will last for several years, possibly even outliving you and your children. They will become a permanent feature of your garden and, unlike rows of cabbages and carrots, there will be fewer unseemly gaps after you have collected your harvest.

If you are lucky enough to have the space, you can set aside an area of your garden as an allotment, kitchen garden or potager. Berries are an important element of these gardens because, along with tree fruits, they will form the permanent structure. Allotments and kitchen gardens were traditionally laid out in straight rows (largely for ease of planting and weeding and to maximize the sunlight each plant received), while potagers were more ornamental. The word comes from the seventeenth century French *jardin potager* meaning 'a garden providing vegetables for the pot', but these productive areas were always beautifully laid out, with intricate patterns, arches and decorative walkways. Flowers were often mixed in too, both for cutting and to maximize the beauty of the garden.

If you don't have that sort of space (and most of us don't), you can still easily grow berries in amongst your ornamental plants and many plants grown for ornamental purposes have crops of delicious berries as well. You can create a very attractive garden using nothing but berries. Many berries have beautiful spring blossom, plants such as blueberries turn amazing shades of red and orange in the autumn and some blackberry hybrids have striking red or white stems in winter.

The lack of a garden need not stop you growing berries. A window box, a hanging basket or a couple of planters by the front door can give you a delicious harvest. Many berries grow just as well in containers as in open soil and, for those with specific soil requirements, containers may be the easiest way to grow them.

Growing most berries is very easy, but as with all fruiting plants they will need a certain amount of care and attention throughout the year. Below are some general points to be aware of, specific information on the individual berries then follows.

Unless specified, plant dimensions refer to final height and spread.

GROWING BERRIES

The Berry Year

Autumn is the time to plan your garden. It is the best time to prepare the soil and plant many berries. In following years it will also be the time of harvest, when you collect the last of your crops.

Winter is the dormant time for most berries. Many of the plants lose their leaves and, to a certain extent, they hibernate (we know how they feel). That said, for most berries a reasonably cold winter is a good thing, killing off unwanted bugs and preparing the plants for the following year. This is the time to prune many berry bushes.

In spring you need to keep an eye out for any potentially damaging frosts. This is the time when the plants wake up, pollination occurs and the fruits begin to form. You should feed the plants now and mulch once the ground has warmed up.

Summer is the time for watering, feeding, guarding against birds and, of course harvesting.

Below is a list of the times you can expect your plants to be most productive. Remember this will vary according to the conditions in your garden and the particular cultivar you grow.

Late spring: gooseberries, honeyberries (haskaps), alpine strawberries

Early summer: gooseberries, honeyberries (haskaps), alpine strawberries, summer strawberries

Berries

Mid summer: blackberries, hybrid brambles, bilberries, blueberries, gooseberries, lingonberries, mulberries, summer raspberries, alpine strawberries, summer strawberries

Late summer: blackberries, hybrid brambles, bilberries, blueberries, goji berries, gooseberries, garden huckleberries, Japanese wineberries, mulberries, summer raspberries, alpine strawberries, perpetual strawberries

Early autumn: blackberries, hybrid brambles, bilberries, blueberries, cranberries, goji berries, garden huckleberries, Japanese wineberries, lingonberries, autumn raspberries, alpine strawberries, perpetual strawberries

Mid autumn: cranberries, goji berries, autumn raspberries, alpine strawberries, perpetual strawberries

Late autumn to the first frosts: goji berries, autumn raspberries

Times for *Gaylussacia* and *Vaccinium* huckleberries and many of the ornamental plants on page 104-108 vary with the particular cultivar.

THE SOIL

Throughout this section you will read, time and time again, that plants like soil that is moisture-retentive *and* free-draining. This may seem an impossible combination, but what it means is that the soil should be able to hold sufficient water for the plant's needs without ever becoming waterlogged. In reality, this is a luxury most of us don't have in our gardens; chalk drains too quickly, clay too slowly. To improve almost any soil, dig in plenty of organic matter (garden compost or well-rotted manure) to the area a couple of weeks before you plant. It may seem dull, but the condition of your soil is one of the most important things you should consider before planting any fruits. Many plants can withstand cold temperatures, but don't like sitting in soggy soil in winter.

Trellis for Canes

Berries such as blackberries, summer-fruiting raspberries and many of the hybrid brambles grow on long canes which can quickly become unruly and need to be supported (think of them as your garden's teenagers). You can either grow them against a wall or fence or along a free-standing trellis. A system of single or, preferably, doubled posts should be fixed 3 m / 10 ft apart. Three strands of strong wire stretched in between the posts (heights: 75 cm / 30 in, 1.1 m / 40 in and 1.5 m / 5 ft) will provide a good basic framework. Twine or extra wire can be woven between the main wires for added support.

Choosing the Berries

Put very simply, most individual berries are separate species (written as a Latin name in two parts; *Rubus fruticosus* or blackberry). Once the full name has been given, and the meaning is clear, the genus, or first part, is given as a letter (*R. fruticosus*). These species are then further divided into cultivars, or varieties usually cultivated by man (written with capitals and in inverted commas; *R. fruticosus* 'Loch Ness'). You may find fruits for sale simply labelled by their common name, but it is worth seeking out different cultivars as it is here that you get the refinements such as early or late harvests, particularly tasty fruits or compact plants. Heritage varieties have historical interest and can be worth growing, but beware as they may be less productive or more disease-prone than more recent cultivars. Plants are increasingly bred with in-built resistance to pests and diseases and these will make your gardening easier and your plants healthier. Different species can vary considerably in terms of hardiness however, a lot will depend on the conditions in your garden (aspect, shelter, soil) so hardiness ratings should be used as a guide, rather than an inflexible rule.

While members of the *Rubus* genus (blackberries, raspberries etc.) can be accused of interbreeding, berries in the *Vaccinium* genus can be accused of having too many common names. Blueberries, bilberries, cranberries, lingonberries and some huckleberries belong within this group and bilberries alone have at least ten different names in Britain, according to where you are in the country. Matters become even more confused when you include American common names. *V. deliciosum* is the cascade bilberry to some, the blue huckleberry to others or even the cascade huckleberry. Always check the Latin name so you know exactly what you are buying.

BUYING PLANTS

When you buy your plants, they will either be bare-rooted or in a container. Bare-rooted plants often come from specialist nurseries, where your choice of cultivar may be greater. They are sold or sent out when the plants are dormant, any time from late autumn to early spring. They need to be soaked in water for half an hour as soon as you get them and then planted, or at least heeled into a patch of soil, so that they do not dry out. Container plants can be bought at any time of year, but almost all berry plants are best planted in autumn or spring, when the soil is not too cold or wet. Always buy plants from a reputable source and check that they are certified free of viruses.

PLANTING

The hole must be large enough to accommodate the roots easily. The roots of container-grown plants should be gently teased out from the rootball so that they grow into the surrounding soil and do not just grow round in circles following the line of the original pot. All shrubs benefit from the addition of mycorrhizal fungi when planted. This is a natural fungus, which is available as a powder and allows the plant to take up nutrients from the soil more easily. The plant will slowly develop its own mycorrhizae, but by adding some at the beginning you will give the plant a hugely increased chance of settling in and thriving. Always follow the instructions on the packet.

Mulching, Feeding and Watering

In spring, sprinkle general-purpose feed around berry plants. Most berry plants also benefit from a layer of mulch in the spring, once the soil has warmed up. You should weed and water first and then apply a 5-8 cm / 2-3 in layer of garden compost or well-rotted manure. Avoid using mushroom compost round acidic-loving plants such as blueberries or cranberries as it is naturally alkaline and will reduce the acidity that they need to survive. Always leave a 5 cm / 2 in gap around any stems, otherwise they may rot.

Regular watering is vital while the actual berries are growing. If a plant is under any sort of stress it will simply drop its berries. This safeguards the plant for another year, but means you will lose your crop; more berries won't grow that year. Plants such as blueberries and cranberries have particular needs but, as a general guide, strawberries need watering every couple of days and most other berry plants will need a good soaking once a week. Plants in containers will probably need watering most days during summer.

A little liquid seaweed on the run-up to harvesting is appreciated by most plants; a couple of feeds two weeks apart will be sufficient for most berries growing in open soil. Plants growing in containers have special requirements, see page 102-104.

Training and Pruning

Many of the hybrid blackberry-raspberry crosses grow very fast and need to be tied in regularly; otherwise you risk your neat berry patch turning into a thorny, impenetrable jungle. Most berries need some sort of regular pruning, at the very least, the removal of the 'three Ds' – dead, diseased and damaged branches. Specific pruning details are given under each berry.

Netting

If you want to maximize your crops you will need to net most berries to prevent birds eating them before you can harvest them. A well-constructed fruit cage can make a focal point in a large kitchen garden, but often netting can look messy or straggly, especially if you grow fruit mixed in with ornamental plants, so you need to balance aesthetics with practicality. One option is to share your crop and appreciate the birds that are attracted to the garden. William Lawson in his book *A New Orchard and Garden* of 1656 is in favour of a certain amount of birdsong but also recommends, 'a Stone-Bow, a Piece, especially if you have a Musket, or a sparrow-hawk'. We tend to share our crops one year, become exasperated with birds beating us to the berries, and net the following year – not a very organized approach but at least, in the long run, we get birds and fruit. It is entirely up to you. If you do use it, the netting should be fairly thick, so that birds do not become entangled in it.

WEEDS, PESTS AND DISEASES

It may seem as though the garden is full of nasties waiting to destroy your crops and you must be in a state of constant combat-readiness, but if your plants are strong and healthy they will be able to withstand most onslaughts. They will be able to do this better if their beds are kept weed-free as the weeds can smother small plants and will compete for any available water and nutrients.

Since you are going to eat the fruit it seems pointless to spray it with a mass of chemicals; the best way to ward off danger is to keep an eye on your plants so you can deal with any problems before they become serious. Pick off pests as soon as they appear, cut away any diseased parts and give seaweed extract to boost the plant's natural defences. Biological controls can be useful against specific pests. If you need to use chemicals make sure you choose the correct one and always follow the manufacturer's instructions. Many new cultivars have been bred to have a natural resistance to pests and diseases and, if possible, these are the plants to choose.

Companion Planting

Certain plants can be used to help keep your garden healthy naturally. Some of these companion plants will help fight diseases; others will attract helpful predators such as ladybirds, hoverflies and lacewings that will eat some of the pests threatening your crop. There is much debate as to how much good companion planting does, but one thing is certain; it does no harm. Many people believe that companion plants are natural partners in the kitchen as well as the flower bed and base recipes around these herb/berry combinations. These plants will make the area round your berries healthier and more attractive. Some of the most useful plants are:

Borage (*Borago officinalis*) is reputed to increase strawberry yields.

Chives (*Allium schoenoprasum*) will help against mildew and blackspot.

Tansy (*Tanacetum vulgare*) will deter fruit moths.

Lemon balm (*Melissa officinalis*) reduces the risk of fungal disease.

Gaillardias (*Gaillardia* spp.), poached egg flower (*Limnanthes douglasii*), phacelia (*Phacelia tanacetifolia*), pot marigolds (*Calendula officinalis)* and cow parsley (*Anthriscus sylvestris*) all attract beneficial insects.

The *Allium* genus will deter pests and attract beneficial insects.

French marigolds (*Tagetes*) and herbs such as rosemary, thyme, sage and lavender deter predators by disorientating them or masking the scent of the fruit with their own fragrance.

Single flowers attract the vitally-needed pollinating insects such as bees.

BLACKBERRIES AND HYBRID BRAMBLES

Picking brambles should be part of everyone's childhood memories; eating the fruits in the sunshine, your fingers becoming with increasingly purple-stained as you pick. Almost wherever you live you can find blackberries growing wild in hedgerows, parks or even abandoned building sites. It may seem pointless to grow your own, but cultivated blackberries are a great addition to wild ones, not a replacement for them. The cultivated fruits tend to be larger and firmer and selective breeding over the years means you can also grow berries such as tayberries and loganberries which are harder to find growing wild.

Blackberries and raspberries are extraordinarily promiscuous and have interbred (both naturally and at the hand of man) to produce a huge range of hybrid berries. Loganberries are large, sharp and perfect for cooking, tayberries are huge and sweet, with tummelberries being similar but hardier. Boysenberries, youngberries, marionberries, sunberries and veitchberries give further variations. Japanese wineberries and dewberries are separate species but grow similarly. They all have attractive flowers like miniature wild roses and will remain productive for about fifteen to twenty years.

POSITION

All these berries are easy to grow and will give you delicious fruit for little effort. They are self-fertile so you only need one plant. Be wary though, as some can be rampant and will try to take over your garden. All the hybrid berries need a sunny spot, although blackberries are not so fussy and will also crop well in light shade. All need a sheltered site as strong winds can damage the canes and will deter the necessary pollinating insects. Blackberries don't mind how poor the soil is; to get the best results from hybrid berries dig in well-rotted manure or garden compost before planting. They are all hardy in Britain and in the USA they grow in zones 5-9, depending on the cultivar.

Planting, Care and Harvesting

Blackberries and hybrid brambles can look unprepossessing when you buy them; a single short cane, either in a pot or bare-rooted. Both are best planted between early winter and mid spring, at a time when the ground is not frozen or waterlogged. The planting distances below may seem huge, but these are large plants and do best when given plenty of space. Most hybrids are less vigorous than blackberries.

Compact varieties: 1.8-2.5 m / 6-8 ft

Vigorous varieties: 3-4 m / 10-13 ft

Very vigorous varieties: 4-6 m / 13-20 ft

Feed the plants in late winter or early spring with a general-purpose fertilizer and then, once the soil has warmed up, weed and mulch. Water the plants if the summer is dry, especially once the fruits begin to ripen. Blackberries probably won't need netting, although you may want to protect hybrid berries. All these berries should be left to ripen fully on the plant. The fruits should come away easily and, as with all berries, are best picked in the morning or early evening, once any dew has dried, but out of the direct heat of the sun.

Pruning and Training

All these berries fruit on one-year old canes. During summer, as the new canes grow up it pays to separate them from the previous year's canes which will bear fruit that season. You can either tie the new canes in up the centre of the plant, or to either side or spread them to one side. The first two methods are best unless you have a vast amount of space; the third method means that each year your plant will spread in a different direction and this is only really practicable if you have the plants growing along a hugely long trellis. In autumn, after harvesting you should cut all the stems which have fruited down to ground level and spread out the new canes which will give you the following year's harvest. All these berries grow fast and can easily become straggly if you don't keep them neatly tied in to a framework of wires.

Propagating

Any new shoots will grow roots which can be used to make new plants. During summer, simply bury the tip of a new shoot in the soil and by the end of the year it will have grown roots and can be cut away from the main plant. You can then leave it and transplant it in spring or overwinter it in a pot.

Problems

These berries are usually fairly trouble free. Powdery mildew can be a problem, but can usually be avoided by ensuring good air circulation around the plant. Water and mulch to ensure the soil does not dry out and cut away any badly affected stems.

A Selection of Blackberry Cultivars
(*Rubus fruticosus*)

'**Black Butte**': This cultivar comes from the western United States and is reasonably compact. It bears huge, tasty berries (twice the size of most other blackberries) from mid summer onwards.

'**Loch Ness**': This thornless cultivar is reasonably small and gives high yields of good fruit. It is tolerant of most conditions and the stout canes don't need that much support.

'**Reuben**': This spine-free cultivar is tolerant of most soils and will grow in sun or shade. The dark berries ripen early and are well-flavoured. It has a neat, upright habit and, given good conditions, will produce berries on the current year's growth.

'**Waldo**': This is a compact and thornless cultivar which produces large and delicious berries.

A Selection of Hybrid Brambles

Most of these plants fruit from mid to late summer onwards. Names in brackets indicate how the plant is most commonly written.

Boysenberries (*R.* 'Boysenberry')
These are probably a cross between a loganberry, a raspberry, a dewberry and a blackberry, but are now often listed as a blackberry cultivar. They were found in the 1920s growing on a derelict farm in California which had belonged to a Rudolph Boysen. Walter Knott, a berry expert, rescued the plants and began selling the berries in 1932. The fruits are large and taste similar to old-fashioned wild blackberries. They are more drought-tolerant than most other hybrids and, increasingly, thornless varieties are available.

Dewberries (*R. caesius*)
These are a separate species and are particularly common in America where they are also known as a trailing blackberries. The berries are a blue-grey colour and have good flavour.

Hildaberries (*R.* 'Hildaberry')
These are a cross between a boysenberry and a tayberry, but are now usually listed as a blackberry cultivar. They were raised by an amateur breeder and are charmingly named after his wife. The flowers are large, as are the rounded red berries.

Japanese wineberries see page 101.

King's Acre Berry (*R.* 'King's Acre Berry')
These are a raspberry-blackberry cross, with blackberry-tasting fruits.

Loganberries (*R.* x *loganbaccus*)
These resulted from a chance cross between blackberries and raspberries in the garden of J. H. Logan, a judge in nineteenth-century California with an interest in fruit breeding. He was trying to improve blackberries by crossing different cultivars, but in fact ended up with a far more interesting fruit. The large berries have a wonderful flavour, but are tart and best suited for cooking.

'LY 59': Although the name lacks charm, this is a vigorous and tough cultivar, tolerant of most conditions. It bears large, well-flavoured fruits, but has a lot of thorns to contend with.

'LY 654': This is a thornless loganberry, which is less vigorous than 'LY 59'. The fruits need to be left to ripen fully on the plant to get the best flavour.

Marionberries (*R.* 'Marionberry')
These are actually the blackberry cultivar 'Marion', but they frequently sold as a hybrid berry. Like many blackberries it probably has mixed parentage and almost certainly includes some loganberry ancestors, which account for the sharp taste of the berries.

Nectaberries (*R.* 'Nectaberry')
These are a boysenberry cultivar with well-flavoured berries.

Olallieberries (*R.* 'Olallieberry')
These were raised in Oregon and are a cross between a loganberry and a youngberry. They are frequently marketed as the cultivar 'Olallie'.

Salmonberries (*R. spectabilis*)
These are a blackberry-raspberry cross with large yellowy-orange berries. The plants are native to the west coast of North America and got their name because the Native Americans used to eat the berries with salmon.

Silvanberries / Sylvanberries (*R. 'Silvan'*)

These are a raspberry-blackberry cross from Australia, with boysenberry, loganberry, marionberry and youngberry ancestors. They are sometimes listed as the blackberry cultivar 'Silvan'. The fruits are large, and a lovely glossy dark red, but the stems have vicious thorns.

Sunberries (*R. 'Sunberry'*)

These are a recent hybrid bred at East Malling in Kent and are a blackberry-raspberry cross with a long harvesting period of loganberry-like fruits. The problem for most gardeners is that the plants are very rampant and extremely prickly. The common name can lead to confusion as there is also a species of *Solanum* commonly called sunberries, which are totally different berries. See page 99.

Tayberries (*R.* Tayberry Group)

These are another cross between a raspberry and a blackberry which were bred in Scotland in the 1960s and named after the River Tay. The blackberry flavour dominates and the large berries ripen to a deep red with a deliciously sweet/sharp taste. The plants are reasonably vigorous, but this is one of the best hybrids to choose. They are usually simply labelled as tayberries, rather than a specific cultivar. 'Buckingham' is a thornless cultivar which bears large fruits.

Thimbleberries (*R. parviflorus*)

These berries are native to North America and are also known as flowering raspberries, salmonberries or snow brambles. They have large flowers, despite the Latin *parviflorus* meaning 'small-flowered'. Like true raspberries the berries pull away from the central cone, coming away as a thimble shape. We like them but Henry David Thoreau describes them as 'an honest and homely berry, without much flavour, but wholesome and firm'.

Tummelberries (*R. 'Tummelberry'*)

These are a cross between two tayberries which were bred in Scotland. They are a much hardier plant than their parents and will cope on exposed sites. The berries are not as sweet and ripen slightly later.

Veitchberries (*R.* 'Veitchberry')
A raspberry-blackberry cross with stout canes, these were first produced in 1925 and named after the nurserymen J Veitch and Sons. The large, well-flavoured fruit tastes in between a blackberry and a loganberry and is particularly attractive to birds.

Wyeberries (*R.* 'Wyeberry' or *R.* 'Wye Berry')
These are a raspberry-blackberry cross which were bred at the University of Maryland. The fruits taste of a mixture of raspberries and boysenberries and grow on thorny canes.

Youngberries (*R.* 'Youngberry')
These are a raspberry-blackberry-dewberry cross, bred by Byrnes M. Young, a Louisiana businessman, in 1905. The berries are long and deep red when ripe, with a similar but sweeter taste to loganberries. The canes tend to trail. 'Thornless Youngberry' is the cultivar to choose.

BLUEBERRIES AND BILBERRIES

Blueberries are easy and rewarding to grow. They have attractive ivory, white, or occasionally pink, bell-shaped flowers in spring, followed by delicious, deep purply-blue fruits in summer. In autumn the foliage turns spectacular shades of red and orange. The bushes are mostly quite compact and many cultivars are perfect for growing in containers making them ideal for small gardens. The plants can be slow to settle in but, once established, they will fruit for twenty years or more.

In theory many blueberries are self-fertile, but you will get a more reliable crop if you grow two or three different cultivars which flower at the same time. They don't take up much room and this will also give you a longer and better harvest.

While blueberries come from North America, bilberries (also called blaeberries, whortleberries, whinberries and a host of other local names) are native to the acidic heaths and moors of Europe. They form low-growing shrubs which require the same conditions as blueberries. The berries are small and tart, but intensely flavoured and are the traditional berry for the French *Tarte aux Myrtilles* (see page 145).

Position

The most important thing with blueberries and bilberries is to get the soil correct. It should be rich, free-draining, moisture-retentive and, above all, acidic. Dig in plenty of organic matter and add grit to improve the drainage if necessary. This is one of the times when it is worth checking the pH of your soil; it should be 4-5.5. If it is 8 or over you will need to grow the berries in containers with specialist potting compost. These berries prefer a sheltered and sunny spot, although they will tolerate dappled shade.

Planting, Care and Harvesting

Both are best planted in spring, although you can plant container-grown plants at any time. Add specialist mycorrhizal fungi to help the plant establish itself. As a rough guide, the bushes should be planted 1.2-1.5 m / 4-5 ft apart.

They are hardy (USDA zones 3-10 depending on the cultivar) but some cultivars flower early and may need protection from frost. Simply drape horticultural fleece over the plant if a hard frost is forecast while the plant is in blossom.

In spring give an acid-based feed and mulch well with an acidic mix – pine needles, bracken or bark chips make a good base. Check the pH and, if necessary, add sulphur chips or sprinkle sulphate of ammonia over the soil.

Keep the plants well-watered, especially if you are growing them in containers. The soil should be damp, but not water-logged. Most tap water contains lime, so ideally save rainwater, which is naturally acidic, and use that for watering.

You may need to net the fruit to safeguard your harvest. You should wait to pick the fruit until they develop a slightly dusty-looking bloom; they will then be fully ripe.

Pruning and Training

Blueberries don't really need much pruning but, once the plant is established, you can thin the bush in winter. Cut away the 'three Ds' and any branches that cross through the centre of the plant, cutting back to an upward or outward-facing bud. Each year remove two or three of the older branches that have fruited, as branches over three years old don't fruit so well. Bilberries rarely need pruning.

Propagating

You can take softwood cuttings in midsummer (see Glossary, page 207).

Problems

Apart from the fussiness regarding soil and the need to be fed and watered regularly, blueberries and bilberries don't really have many problems.

Lime-induced chlorosis
This is common where the soil is not sufficiently acidic and the lime present prevents the plant taking up the necessary elements. The leaves will turn yellow, indicating a lack of manganese or iron. Use a special iron feed (sequestered or chelated), following the instructions.

A Selection of Blueberries and Bilberries

Blueberries (*Vaccinium cyanoccocos*) divide into highbush (*V. corymbosum*), lowbush (*V. angustifolium* and *V. myrtilloides,* native to Canada) and rabbit-eye (*V. ashei*) plants. Highbush or northern highbush plants grow into tall shrubs and produce large crops. They can withstand cold winters and in fact need a period of cold weather to flower and fruit well. Lowbush tolerate low temperatures, but tend not to be quite so prolific. Rabbit-eyes and southern highbush blueberries (hybrids of northern and rabbit-eyes) aren't as hardy and prefer temperate climates. There are also 'half-high' plants which are crosses between highbush and lowbush. Most commercially available blueberries in Britain are highbush, although confusingly, some varieties are reasonably small. In America the cultivars are also differentiated by the type to accommodate the climactic variations. By choosing different cultivars it is possible to have fruit throughout the summer.

Bilberries (*V. myrtillus*) are simply sold as the species.

A Selection of Blueberry Cultivars *Vaccinium* spp.

'**Bluecrop**': This grows into a neat upright shape and is suitable for containers. It crops reliably and the large, well-flavoured, slightly tart fruits are followed by good autumn colour. The plants have good disease-resistance.

'**Earliblue**': This is a larger bush than 'Bluecrop', but equally disease-resistance. The pale blue berries are borne on long, arching stems and are one of the first to ripen.

'**Herbert**': This is one of the best-flavoured cultivars. The dark blue berries grow on large, upright plants.

'**Top Hat**': This compact cultivar is good for containers. The fruits aren't particularly large, but are well-flavoured and are followed by splendid autumn colour. It is one of the most reliably self-fertile cultivars.

CRANBERRIES AND LINGONBERRIES

Cranberries (bounceberries) and lingonberries (cowberries) form attractive, evergreen low bushes with pretty pink flowers. They are easy to grow as long as you can provide the acidic boggy conditions similar to their natural habitat. Lingonberries are more compact and sometimes produce two crops of tart but flavoursome berries, one in mid summer and another in early autumn.

These plants are self-fertile so you need only grow one, but they look better as a spreading group.

Position

As with blueberries, the soil is crucial. It must be moist and acidic, ideally with a pH of 5-6 for cranberries, 4-5 for lingonberries. They will do well in boggy soil; a patch in between the blueberry beds and a pond is ideal (if you have such a place). They are very hardy and can be grown in full sun or dappled shade.

Planting, Care and Harvesting

The plants will be container-grown and can be planted at any time of year, although spring is best. Position them 30-45 cm / 12-18 in apart to allow the plants to spread and form a carpet.

Check the pH every spring and add sulphur chips if necessary. A weak ericaceous feed will also help. Water with rainwater and ensure the soil is always moist. A mulch of lime-free, horticultural grit or sharp sand will prevent water evaporating. Lingonberries don't need quite such damp conditions, but should not be allowed to dry out.

Birds are not usually a problem so you shouldn't need to net the fruits. Pick them before any hard frosts. Ripe cranberries will bounce if dropped, hence the common name bounceberries.

Pruning and Training

After fruiting trim the plants lightly to keep them compact. Every two or three years thin some of the stems in spring to prevent the plants becoming congested.

Propagating

Dig up an established clump in mid autumn and gently separate the plant, discarding the woody centre. Divide into smaller plants and replant or pot up in ericaceous compost, watering well.

Problems

Problems are more likely to be due to lime in the soil or dryness, rather than pests or diseases. See blueberry problems on page 75.

A Selection of Cranberries and Lingonberries

European cranberries (*Vaccinium oxycoccos*)
These bear small fruits with a tart taste.

American cranberries (*V. macrocarpon*)
Also known as the large cranberry, these are the most commonly grown commercially.

Bog cranberries (*V. oxycoccos* syn. *Oxycoccos palustris*)
These are the most common wild cranberries, especially in Britain where they are often just called cranberries.

Lingonberries (*V. vitis-idaea*) are simply sold as the species.

Highbush cranberries (*Viburnum triloba*)
These are not a true cranberries but the fruit is similar and can be eaten in the same ways, raw or cooked.

A SELECTION OF CRANBERRY CULTIVARS *Vaccinium* spp.

'**Early Black**': This American cultivar bears large, crimson berries which ripen earlier than most other cultivars. The plants grow into neat hummocks.

'**Pilgrim**': The bright red berries have excellent flavour. The plant is evergreen but turns bronze in autumn.

GOOSEBERRIES

Gooseberries are well worth growing. Once they were a common hedgerow plant, but now it is very rare to find them growing in the wild (deserted kitchen gardens are probably your best bet). Only a few varieties of the berries are ever available to buy and then only for a short time; blink and you are liable to have missed them. They divide into culinary and dessert fruits; the culinary ones are too sour to eat raw, but make delicious pies, fools, jams and curds, while dessert fruits can be eaten straight from the plant. In his book *The Anatomy of Dessert* (1929), Edward Bunyard describes dessert gooseberries as 'the fruit par excellence for consumption'. Many cultivars will give you a crop of culinary fruits early in the season when you thin the berries and then dessert fruits as the remaining berries ripen fully. All gooseberries are self-fertile, so you only need one plant, although once you start growing these delicious fruits you may well find yourself wanting several different cultivars. Gooseberries can be green, yellow, pink or red and vary in size from a marble to a hen's egg. Some are hairy, but never excessively so.

You can grow the plants as bushes, standards or cordons. Bushes have short trunk (10-15 cm / 4-6 in), with stems that fan out into a goblet shape, which can reach up to 2 m / 6 ft. The trunk allows air to circulate round the plant and makes weeding and mulching easier. Standards are simply a goblet grown on a longer trunk, typically 1 m / 3 ft tall. The weight of the top means that standards need stout staking. Cordons, double cordons or fans need careful pruning, but give a good crop in a small space.

Gooseberries are hardy in Britain and in the USA they will grow in zones 3-7, but do best in zones 3-5.

Position

Gooseberries are tough, but for a good crop they should be planted in a sheltered spot, in fertile, well-drained soil. Although gooseberries don't like their roots in soggy soil you should avoid planting them in dry, shallow soil as that will increase the risk of American gooseberry mildew. A little shade won't matter and they can be trained against a north-facing wall or planted beneath fruit trees. A slightly exposed site is fine; a through breeze will deter pests and the air flow will reduce the risk of mildew. As a rough guide you should allow 1.2-1.5 m / 4-5 ft between bushes or standards and 45 cm / 18 in between double cordons.

Planting, Care and Harvesting

Dig in plenty of garden compost or well-rotted manure and add a general granular fertilizer to the area a couple of weeks before you plant gooseberries. They should be planted in late autumn; for bare-rooted plants this is the only time; with container-grown plants you have a little more latitude and they can be planted at any time, but autumn will give the plant time to settle before it starts producing flowers and fruit. Plant so the soil level on the stem is level with the ground. Then water well. On a bush you should then cut all the stems back by half, to an outward-facing bud; this will give your plant the open goblet-shape that it needs to be healthy.

Gooseberries flower early and can be at risk from late frosts. If you think there is going to be a hard frost while the plant is in bloom, cover it overnight with fleece, which will protect the flowers. Every spring, sprinkle with a general fertilizer containing sulphate of potash. Avoid feeding gooseberries with high-nitrogen fertilizers as this will stimulate leaf growth and increase the risk of mildew. Then mulch with garden compost or well-rotted manure. The plants should remain productive for ten to fifteen years.

Dessert gooseberries should be thinned in late spring or early summer. Remove half the fruits. This may seem a lot to cut away, but it will give you a harvest of better berries later and you can use the small fruits for cooking. Bushes may need supporting with canes and twine to stop the branches sagging and you should tie in the shoots on cordons and fans as they grow. Water in summer while the plants are fruiting to ensure the roots do not dry out. Culinary gooseberries can be harvested as soon as they are big enough to use; some cultivars can be picked in late spring. Dessert gooseberries should be left to ripen on the bush and will be ready to pick in mid summer. You will need to net dessert varieties if you want to safeguard your crop.

Pruning and Training

You should prune in winter while the plants are dormant. When pruning, bear in mind that gooseberries fruit on the stems of the previous season and on spurs along the older branches. Cut away any shoots growing out at the base of the trunk and remove any suckers that have grown up around the plant. For bushes remove the 'three Ds' and cut away any stems congesting the centre so you get an open wineglass shape. Shorten the main stems by a third to half, back to an inward-facing bud to encourage upright growth. Cut the side shoots back to 5-7.5 cm / 2-3 in to an outward-facing bud. In mid summer, after harvesting, shorten all the side shoots to about five leaves.

To grow the plant as a standard, tie a single stem to a sturdy cane (90 cm / 3 ft). Remove any shoots that appear on the lower part of the stem and pinch out the shoots at the top to encourage them to produce a bushy head. You then prune in the same way as a bush.

To train a double cordon, tie two stems onto a trellis, spreading them so that they are both growing upright, 30 - 45 cm / 12 - 18 in apart. Fans can be created by spreading out several stems. Pruning single or double cordons or fans is the same. In winter prune the main leader(s) by a quarter of the previous summer's growth and tie in. Cut the side shoots back to 2.5 cm / 1 in (1 or 2 buds). In mid summer, after harvesting, shorten all the side shoots to about five leaves. Once the leader(s) reach the height you want, cut the top to prevent any more upward growth.

Propagating

You can increase your supply of plants by taking hardwood cuttings in autumn (see the Glossary, page 207)

Problems

Gooseberries can be attacked by squirrels and birds, especially bullfinches, which will eat the buds before they have even formed fruits. To minimize the risk of various mildews and fungi, ensure the plants are kept well-watered, but not soggy, and that the air circulation round and through the plants is good.

American gooseberry mildew
When this occurs the leaves and stems become covered with a white fungus, which can also appear on the fruit. You can spray with a fungicide, but prevention is better. Ideally, choose cultivars with some resistance, such as 'Greenfinch', 'Hinnonmaki Red', 'Invicta' or 'Martlet'. Wipe the fungus off the fruits (they are fine to eat) and cut away affected shoots after harvesting. Improve the air circulation and in spring feed with sulphate of potash rather than a general fertilizer.

Magpie moth

The caterpillars appear in late spring or early summer and have distinctive black, white and orange markings. Remove them by hand before they have a chance to eat the leaves.

Gooseberry sawfly

The pale green caterpillars have black spots and can strip a plant of its leaves in a matter of days. Check the undersides of the leaves regularly from late spring onwards for eggs and destroy any infected leaves (don't compost them). Remove any caterpillars by hand.

Potash deficiency

This will show as brown edges to the leaves. Apply a feed of sulphate of potash in late winter. (15 g per square metre / ½ oz per square yard).

Blister rust

Gooseberries (and other plants on the *Ribes* genus) can be carriers of this disease. It rarely affects the plants themselves, but can travel to any nearby white pines, where it is fatal. This is why the growing of gooseberries is restricted in some areas of the United States although, increasingly, rust-resistant cultivars are available.

A SELECTION OF THE GOOSEBERRIES AND THEIR CLOSE RELATIONS

European gooseberries (*Ribes uva-crispa*)

The cultivars of this species have large, well-flavoured fruits.

American gooseberries (*R. hirtellum*)

The plants in this species tend to be more resistant to powdery mildew and, although the berries are smaller than the European gooseberries, the crops tend to be heavier.

Many cultivars are a combination of the two.

Jostaberries (*R.* x *culverwellii*)

These are a hybrid which was created when a gooseberry was crossed with a blackcurrant in Germany. The deep purple berries are smaller than true gooseberries and taste of a combination of the two parents. As with gooseberries, they can be cooked when young or eaten straight from the plant when fully ripe. The plants are tough, thornless and resistant to most diseases.

Worcesterberries (*R.* 'Worcesterberry')

These are a native American species, but they grow in the same way as a gooseberries and are frequently wrongly listed as a cultivar or hybrid. The fruits ripen to a deep, dusky red, but rarely become sweet enough to eat raw. It is resistant to gooseberry mildew, but beware the vicious thorns. 'Black Velvet' is a cross between a Worcesterberry and a gooseberry and bears dark red berries.

A Selection of Gooseberry Cultivars *Ribes* spp.

'**Hinnonmaki Red**': This is a very hardy, slow-growing cultivar, making it ideal for both cold and small gardens. It also has good disease resistance. The culinary/dessert berries ripen to dark red. Also available 'Hinnonmaki Green' and 'Hinnonmaki Yellow'.

'**Invicta**': This cultivar is thorny, but is mildew-resistant and easy to grow. The large crops of green berries are best used as culinary fruits.

'**Whinham's Industry**': These plants have a neat upright habit and are tolerant of heavy soil and shade. The green culinary berries ripen to dark red dessert fruits. It can be prone to mildew.

RASPBERRIES

Really tasty raspberries only appear fleetingly in shops and markets, but if you grow your own you will be able to harvest delicious fruit from mid summer right up to the first frost. Raspberries collapse when washed so it is really worth growing your own, without any chemicals, so all you will have to do is gently brush away the occasional cobweb. The berries are delicate and do not travel well, the distance from your garden to your kitchen is just about ideal. Growing your own also allows you to sample the more unusual yellow, gold and black raspberries.

Summer-fruiting raspberries grow on long canes whereas the autumn-fruiting varieties form low bushes. Both thrive in cool, damp weather and are easy to grow. They are fully hardy and will grow in USDA zones 3-8, with the summer-fruiting plants being slightly hardier. If you have limited space grow the autumn-fruiting varieties as these are the ones which are harder to buy and often have better flavour. They take up less space and crop for over two months.

The main difference between the two fruits is that summer-fruiting raspberries crop on the previous year's canes, whereas the autumn-fruiting cultivars fruit on the current season's growth. Consequently they require different pruning and it pays to plant them in separate areas so the plants do not intermingle, which they will do, given half a chance. Ideally, you should keep different cultivars a little apart too, but in most gardens this isn't going to be practical space-wise. Both types will be productive for about ten years.

POSITION

Raspberries like well-drained soil, but they need slightly damper conditions than many other berries, so add plenty of organic matter to your soil if it is chalk or sand-based. They do best in soil which is slightly acidic (pH 6-6.5) so, if necessary, add sulphur chips or ericaceous compost before planting.

You should avoid areas with strong winds as the long canes need shelter and, although they are self-fertile, the flowers need to be pollinated by insects. The plants will survive perfectly well in a little shade, but they do best in full sun.

Planting, Care and Harvesting

Raspberries can look unprepossessing when you buy them, a single short cane, either in a pot or bare-rooted. Both container-grown and bare-rooted plants are best planted between early winter and mid spring, at a time when the ground is not frozen or waterlogged.

Weed the area, dig in plenty of well-rotted manure or garden compost and, for summer fruiting varieties erect a support (see page 62). Place the canes 30-40 cm / 12-15 in apart, tease the roots away from the rootball or spread the bare roots out 8 cm / 3 in below the soil, and firm in. Autumn raspberries will flower and fruit in their first year, summer fruiting may flower and fruit on their existing canes or will crop in their second year.

Raspberries have shallow roots so they run the risk of drying out; you should water well twice a week, taking care to water the soil rather than the plants, so as to avoid fungal diseases. In spring, give the plants a general feed and then mulch with garden compost or well-rotted manure. Leave a little gap around each cane to prevent it rotting.

Summer-fruiting plants will need to be netted, this is not usually necessary for autumn-fruiting varieties. The fruits are ripe when they come away easily from the central core.

Pruning and Training

Summer-fruiting varieties
After the harvest, in late summer, you should cut the canes that have fruited down to the ground. New canes, which will fruit the following year, should be growing up. The old canes will be brown at the base, the new ones pale green. Remove any weak-looking stems, leaving 4-5 shoots per plant. If the new canes are unevenly spaced, simply

dig up and move any that are congested, positioning them so they are reasonably evenly spread (ideally 7-10 cm / 3-4 in apart). Tie the new canes into the supports. If they get too tall, cut the canes back to 15 cm / 6 in above the top of the support.

Autumn-fruiting varieties
In mid to late winter cut the canes down to just above the ground and remove any suckers. New canes will grow in spring and fruit in the autumn. Any new canes that look very weak should be cut to ground level in early summer.

PROPAGATING

Suckers will appear round the main plant. If you want more plants, in autumn simply dig up a sucker with some roots attached and plant in a pot to establish itself.

PROBLEMS

Viruses
Raspberries are prone to viruses that are spread by aphids. The foliage will become mottled, the plants will be stunted and the crop poor. Eventually most canes will become affected, which is why it is best to replace canes after about ten years and plant the new canes in a different area.

Diseases
Cane blight (canes turn black at the base) and cane spot (canes develop purple blotches) will kill individual canes. There is no cure, but many cultivars are now available with good resistance. Avoiding over-crowding and ensuring good air circulation will help to minimize these problems.

Lime-induced chlorosis
The leaves will turn yellow, indicating a lack of manganese or iron.

This is common where the soil is not naturally neutral or acidic and the lime present prevents the plant taking up the necessary elements. Each spring you should apply sulphur chips or sulphur powder to the ground or use a special iron feed (sequestered or chelated). Simply follow the manufacturer's instructions.

A Selection of Raspberries

Black raspberries (*R. occidentalis*)
Also known as black caps and, confusingly, thimbleberries (see *Rubus pariflorus* page 72) these are a separate species, native to eastern North America. They look like blackberries, but come away at the core when picked, like other raspberries. The fruits are small and slightly tart. The plants are not as hardy as other raspberries and do not grow suckers, but produce new plants when the tips of the long canes touch the ground and root.

Purple raspberries (*R.* 'Brandywine', *R.* 'Estate', *R.* 'Royalty')
The cultivars are closely related to black raspberries. The plants tend to be very vigorous and are drought tolerant, but less hardy than the red cultivars. Some send up suckers, others root at the tips.

A Selection of Summer-fruiting Raspberry Cultivars (*Rubus idaeus*)

'**Malling Jewel**': These are compact plants, which will tolerate most sites and have good virus resistance. The berries ripen early and although the yields aren't that high, the fruits have very good flavour.

'**Tulameen**': This cultivar was bred in Canada, is very hardy and has good disease resistance. The large, pinky-red berries are well-flavoured and crop over a long period.

'**Valentina**': The berries ripen to an unusual orange-pink colour and are very sweet. The upright canes only have a few spines and have good resistance to pests and diseases.

A Selection of Autumn-fruiting Raspberry Cultivars (*Rubus idaeus*)

'**Allgold**': The yellow berries grow on short, stout canes and are usually ignored by birds (their loss we feel). The canes are spiny, but the fruit is deliciously sweet.

'**Autumn Bliss**': This was one of the first high-yielding autumn-fruiting raspberries and is still one of the best. The sturdy canes are resistant to rot and the bright red berries ripen early. For the best results plant in a sheltered, sunny site.

'**Polka**': This cultivar was bred in Poland and boasts twice the yield plus improved disease resistance. The large red berries ripen early and bridge the gap between the summer and autumn fruiting seasons.

STRAWBERRIES

Strawberries should be a fleeting treat, the first heralds of summer, with luscious red berries dripping juice and flavour. Instead, they are now available for most of the year and, while the berries may still be red, they rarely have the flavour that can instantly conjure up a summer's afternoon listening to the distant thwack of a cricket ball on willow. Growing your own strawberries will allow you to again appreciate summer at its best (even if you hate cricket).

There are three main types of strawberry plant. Summer fruiting (single-crop, June-bearer) strawberries will provide a short, heavy crop in mid summer, whereas perpetual (remontant, everbearer, autumn-fruiting or two-crop) produce smaller yields over a longer period. Day-neutral strawberries will crop within twelve weeks of planting, regardless of the length of day, providing the temperature is sufficiently warm. These clearly involve considerable infrastructure in terms of heated greenhouses or polytunnels and are not really practical for the average gardener. If you are growing strawberries for home consumption, you are better off choosing summer fruiting or perpetual fruits. Part of the joy of most fruit is their fleeting availability; all-year strawberries are never quite as good as they sound. Alpines or wild strawberries are a slightly different plant with a long harvest, producing tiny, jewel-like fruits from early summer to the first frosts.

POSITION

All strawberries do best in full sun and need well-drained soil. Before planting, dig in well-rotted manure or garden compost. If your soil doesn't drain well, plant the strawberries along earthed-up ridges. You could also create raised beds or grow the berries in growing bags; the latter aren't attractive but work well. Avoid areas where potatoes, tomatoes or chrysanthemums have recently grown. Also avoid windy areas as this will deter the necessary pollinating insects. Depending on the cultivar, they can be grown in USDA zones 3-9.

PLANTING, CARE AND HARVESTING

Strawberries are easy and rewarding to grow, but you do need to give them regular attention if you want a good crop. They are easiest bought as bare-rooted or container plants as seeds can be tricky to raise. Freshly-dug runners are available in late summer onwards; in late spring or early summer you may get cold-stored runners, which were stored just below freezing. Either can be a good source and should be planted as soon as you get them.

If you plant summer fruiting or perpetual varieties in late summer to early autumn, you should get a harvest the following year. You should avoid planting during winter or when the soil is wet, but planting in mid to late spring is fine - you will just have to wait till the following year for a decent crop. Cold-stored runners can be planted in late spring or early summer and, if you are lucky, will give you a harvest in late summer or early autumn.

Remove any over-long runners and place the plants 45 cm / 18 in apart, making sure that the crown of the plant is level with the surface of the soil. In a raised bed, with rich soil, you can reduce the distance to 30 cm / 12 in.

Early varieties may need protection from frost; cloches or fleece offer the best protection and can easily be removed once the temperature rises.

The plants are shallow-rooted and need regular water, especially when young or during dry periods. Try to water the surrounding soil, rather than the fruits to reduce the risk of grey mould or botrytis. If you water early in the morning, any splashes of water will evaporate in the daytime sun. If there is a long spell of wet weather it is worth putting cloches over the fruit to act as an umbrella. In early to mid spring apply a general fertilizer and then feed every two weeks during the growing season with a high potash liquid feed such as tomato feed.

Once the berries start to form, they will need a protective mulch, otherwise they will be sitting on the bare earth. You can use purpose-made fibre mats, plastic sheeting or traditional straw. The fibre mats have a hole in the centre and a slit which means they can easily be placed round each plant and are a good choice. Plastic sheeting needs to be stretched taut over the area so pools of water don't collect. The best way is to raise the bed in the centre so it forms a gentle mound and then bury the edges of the plastic under soil. You then cut a cross in the plastic and insert the plant. The advantages are that the soil warms up under the plastic and weeds are suppressed, but the plastic looks unattractive and you really need to install an irrigation system beneath it in order to be able to water the plants effectively. A layer of straw was the traditional form of protection and looks charmingly rustic, but it can encourage slugs. Tuck the straw under the leaves and fruit, leaving a little gap immediately round the stems. Either barley or wheat straw is suitable; you should avoid oat straw as it can contain eelworms.

As soon as the fruits begin to ripen, you will need to spread a net over the plants to prevent birds or squirrels eating your crop. The easiest way is to fix the middle of the netting to posts so it is above the fruits and weigh down the edges with stones, or use a cloche frame and drape the netting over it. Either way, make sure the netting is raised above the plants; otherwise the birds will simply eat the fruits through the mesh. The netting should be fairly thick, so that birds do not become entangled in it.

The optimum time for harvesting the fruit is short so check the fruits every day, picking any fully red berries. They are best eaten the same day.

Pruning and Training

After all the fruits have been picked, remove the protective mulch and cut off any old leaves or unwanted runners. Leave 8 cm / 3 in as this will form the following year's plant.

Propagating

It is easy to propagate new plants; simply allow the runners to form roots and then cut them away from the main plants and replant or pot up for use the following year. Strawberry plants are really only productive for about three to four years, so this is a good way to replenish your stock. Like vegetables, strawberry beds should be rotated every few years so the soil does not become depleted of nutrients or get a build-up of disease. Put new plants into the new site, otherwise you will simply spread any lurking problems to the new area.

Problems

Slugs and snails
There are almost as many ways to deter slugs and snails as there are the slimy creatures themselves. We protect young plants by scattering

grit on the beds. If you are using a raised bed, you can safeguard the whole area easily by putting copper tape round the edges.

Grey mould
This is worst in wet summers and can be caused by allowing water to splash the fruit. Ensure air circulates well round the plants and keep weeds to a minimum.

Viruses
These are spread by aphids so, sooner or later, your plants will probably succumb, although you can reduce the risk by controlling the aphids. Yellow blotched leaves and poor harvests are indicators. Dig out and destroy and affected plants immediately and replace with new virus-free stock.

A Selection of Strawberry Cultivars
(*Fragaria* x *ananassa*)

'**Cambridge Favourite**': This is a traditional summer-fruiting cultivar which is still worth growing. It crops well, has good disease-resistance and the berries have good flavour.

'**Hapil**': These large summer-fruiting berries ripen to a pale orangey-red and are sweetly-flavoured. The plants have an upright habit and do well on light soils.

'**Honoye**': The glossy summer-fruiting red berries ripen early and have excellent flavour. The plants are not particularly vigorous, but give good yields and are disease-resistant.

'**Mara des Bois**': This is by far the best perpetual to grow. The large glossy fruits taste and smell exactly like wild strawberries. The plants are easy to grow and are resistant to powdery mildew.

Alpine or wild strawberries (*Fragaria vesca*) produce tiny jewel-like red or white fruits and are also known as *fraises des bois* or strawberries of the woods. They grow on dainty plants with attractively toothed evergreen leaves and pretty white flowers which appear alongside the berries throughout early summer through to autumn. Within a year the plants will have spread to form a mat and from the second year onwards you should get a good harvest. These berries will never give you a huge crop, but that is not the point; a few, eaten in the garden, on top of a trifle or garnishing a cake, are all you need. Once established, the plants spread readily. They can be used as decorative edging and don't need to be netted. They make good ground cover plants and although they can be invasive, they are so delightful, it scarcely seems to matter.

You can buy plants or grow them from seed. Sow the seeds in late winter and then be patient, they can take 4-6 weeks to germinate. They should be planted out in late spring, 30 cm / 12 in apart. Alpine strawberries are tolerant of most soils, although a little garden compost or well-rotted manure dug in prior to planting will improve the harvest. They like full sun or dappled shade in areas with very hot summers. Mulching will reduce weeds and reduce water loss. You should water well for the first few weeks while the plants settle in and then when the weather is dry. Feed with a liquid feed while they are flowering and fruiting. The plants will be most productive for about four years so it is a good idea to grow a few from seed every other year so your plants are constantly replenished. The only problem is powdery mildew, which can usually be avoided if you keep the plants well watered and thin regularly to stop them becoming congested.

A SELECTION OF ALPINE STRAWBERRY CULTIVARS
(*F. vesca*)

The plants are often simply sold as 'alpines' but, if you get the choice,

'Baron Solemacher' and 'Ruegen' both produce particularly good fruits over a long period.

'**Mignonette**' are usually only available as seeds, but they are easy to grow and have heavy crops of delicious berries.

For looks:

'**Golden Alexandra**' has bright yellowy-green leaves.

'**Multiplex**' has double white flowers.

'**Muricata**', or the Plymouth strawberry, has green flowers, followed by spiny red fruits; more a talking point than a culinary delight.

'**Variegata**' has grey-green leaves with cream edges.

White Strawberries

For most people, strawberries conjure up a picture of bright red fruits. However white berries are available, both as small alpine varieties and pineberries. Pineberries are a hybrid strawberry, resulting from a cross of berries from North and South America. They have white flesh, red seeds and an unusual pineapple taste. The fruits ripen from green to white and are ready to harvest in early summer. They are grown in the same way as ordinary strawberries and have the advantage that birds rarely eat them. Names are confused and the plants often appear as combinations of *F.* x *ananassa* 'Snow White' or *Pineberry* 'White Dream'.

UNUSUAL GARDEN BERRIES

These are berries you might not obviously think of growing, but are some of our favourites. They tend to be hard to find, either in the shops or in the wild, they grow on interesting plants; most are easy to grow and all are delicious.

Goji or Wolf Berries

Goji berries are famed for their health-giving properties and although you can easily buy the dried berries, the plants are worth growing, both for their looks and the harvest of fresh berries. These fresh berries are almost impossible to buy because, like so many others, they don't transport well. They are sweet, juicy and, of course, good for you.

They belong to the potato family (Solanaceae) and originate in the foothills of the Himalayas. Their leaves resemble an olive's and the clusters of trumpet-shaped, purple and white flowers grow into bunches of bright orange-red berries in late summer and autumn. They may be marketed as superfoods from the East, but they have been grown in Britain since the eighteenth century, when they were known as The Duke of Argyll's tea-tree.

The deciduous bushes are hardy (USDA zone 6) and can withstand both cold winters and hot summers. They need to be in a sheltered, sunny spot, but that is really their only requirement; they will grow in any soil and can tolerate drought and even a little shade, although you will get less fruit. Unusually for berries, they are also happy on coastal sites and can be used to anchor sandy soils. They are self-fertile, so you only need one plant.

In most nurseries you will simply be offered the species (*Lycium barbarum, L. chinense*). Follow the general planting instructions (see page 63) and allow plenty of space (1-2 m / 3-6 ft for bushes, 50 cm / 20 in for hedges) between plants. The plants are thorny and tend to flop about, but they make very good informal hedges and can easily be kept in check as bushes. Be prepared to wait a year or so while the plant establishes itself for your first harvest.

You can train the plants along a fence or trellis, it's a bit perilous to do this at first as the stems are thorny, but once the main stems are in place you can easily tie in any new growth. Fruit grows on the previous year's stems, so prune with this in mind. In spring, cut away the 'three Ds', shorten any overlong stems back to a suitable bud and remove a few of the oldest branches which will be less productive. Pull out any unwanted suckers. If the plant gets out of hand you can cut it right back to a 30 cm / 1 ft in early spring, but you will lose that year's harvest.

Aphids can be a problem; spray with a weak solution of liquid soap or seaweed. Birds do like the fruit, but it seems a shame to net the plants as they look so pretty; we tend to share our crop.

Gojis continue to produce flowers while the earlier berries are ripening. This means you get beautiful plants with purple and white flowers, plus orange and red berries from mid summer well into autumn. The berries darken and develop more flavour and sweetness as they ripen; they will come away easily before they are fully ripe so taste a few to check they are at their best. Fully ripe fruit tends to turn black when handled, so one of the best ways to harvest the berries is to put a cloth on the ground (an old sheet is perfect) and give the plant a good shake.

You can grow gojis from seed but the seedlings need molly coddling for a year in a warm temperature, so it is best to buy as plants in the first place. You can increase your stock by taking softwood cuttings in summer, hardwood cuttings in winter, layering the plants in autumn or replanting a sucker in early spring (See Glossary, page 207).

They are particularly suited to cooking in Asian-style soups and poached chicken dishes.

HONEYBERRIES OR HASKAPS

The honeyberry is an edible form of honeysuckle and is also known as the haskap berry or blue honeysuckle. It is native to Siberia and the northern regions of China and Japan, can live for thirty years and is an easy plant to grow. It is the one to choose if you want blueberries without the hassle of creating a bed of acidic soil. In fact they taste how one imagines many blueberries *should* taste, more like the fruit picked off wild bushes. Increasingly, they are becoming available to buy as berries, but the best way to get a good harvest is to grow your own.

The plants form bushes 1.2-2 m / 4-6 ft with bluey-green honeysuckle-like leaves, which turn yellow in autumn. The pale yellow flowers appear in spring, followed by blue oval-shaped fruits, in early to mid summer. They are often the first berries to crop; heralding the approach of summer and its wealth of luscious fruit. When ripe the berries develop a white bloom and crimson flesh. They taste of a wonderful combination of blueberries and blackcurrants, with a little honey to balance the tartness.

They are hardy (USDA zones 3-8), drought-resistant and tolerant of most soils. This, along with, in our opinion, their superior taste, is their huge advantage over blueberries; they don't need acidic soil. The flowers are also hardy, which means you won't lose your harvest to a late frost. They will grow in light shade, but fruit better in sun.

Plant in spring, allowing 1 m / 3 ft spacings for bushes, 50 cm / 20 in for hedges. Some cultivars are self-fertile but you will get a better crop with two or more compatible cultivars. The plants flower in late winter and early spring when there aren't many insects flying about so you will improve your harvest if you hand pollinate the flowers. Simply take a small, soft paint brush and gently brush the flowers, as if you were a bee, visiting the different blooms. Wear a yellow striped jersey to fully embrace the mood.

Water for the first couple of years while the plant settles in, from then on they are fairly tolerant of drought. Feed every spring with a balanced fertilizer and, once the soil warms up, mulch.

You shouldn't need to prune very much. In late winter or early spring remove the 'three Ds'. Also, to prevent overcrowding, cut back a few older stems to a suitable bud. Once the bush has reached the size you want, pinch out the tips to encourage more flowering shoots.

If you want to increase your plants you can collect seeds, take softwood cuttings in summer or hardwood cuttings in late autumn (See Glossary, page 207).

They have very few problems; birds sometimes eat the fruits, but you will probably get away without netting.

The plants are often simply sold under the species names, *Lonicera caerulea* or *L. caerulea* var. *edulis*. Cultivars are being added all the time, so it is worth checking at specialist nurseries. 'Berry Blue' is a large plant with large berries, 'Blue Belle' a smaller plant with very dark berries, 'Blue Forest' has a spreading habit and 'Kamchatka' comes from Siberia and is very hardy (the Ivan Denisovich of the berry world). 'Duo' is sometimes sold as two compatible plants in one pot. Beware that most other honeysuckles are not edible.

See the honeyberry recipes or cook as for blueberries.

HUCKLEBERRIES

There are a number of berries called huckleberries; annual or garden huckleberries (*Solanum scabrum*), eastern or black huckleberries (*Gaylussacia* spp.) and western or cascade huckleberries (*Vaccinium* spp.). To confuse matters further, many blueberries are commonly referred to as huckleberries. The *Solanum* berries make a good talking point because of their links with deadly nightshade, but probably shouldn't be that far up the list of berries to grow. The *Gaylussacia* and *Vaccinium* huckleberries, on the other hand, are plants well worth growing and berries well worth eating; they tend to be similar to blueberries, but often with a better flavour.

Annual or garden huckleberries belong to the potato family and are tender annuals. They should be grown in the same way as tomatoes. Raise plants from seed or buy plants from a reputable source, as they resemble the poisonous deadly nightshade. Sow the seeds in early spring and leave somewhere warm and light; a window sill is fine. When the seedlings reach 12 cm / 5 in pinch out the tips to make the plants bushier. Plant out after the last frost in a sunny, sheltered site. The small purple berries will ripen towards the end of summer. Be aware that the berries are poisonous when green and unripe.

Another berry belonging to the potato family is the sunberry or *S. retroflexum* syn. *S.* x *burbankii* (not to be confused with the bramble *Rubus* 'Sunberry', see page 72). These plants are also called wonderberries and great care must be taken as both names are sometimes applied to the European black nightshade (*S. nigrum*) which is poisonous.

North American *Gaylussacia* huckleberries are similar to blueberries, but have a sharper flavour and a distinctive crunch caused by the seeds. They grow on small bushes (1 m / 3 ft) with leaves which turn wonderful shades of red in autumn. They do best in damp, acidic soil, similar conditions to blueberries. They are hardy (USDA zones 3-8) and will tolerate a certain amount of shade. The black huckleberry (*G. baccata*) is the most common and has small red flowers in spring followed by glossy black fruits. Other huckleberries with good fruits and splendid names are bear huckleberries (*G. ursina*), blue huckleberries (*G. frondosa*), hairy-twig huckleberries (*G. tomentosa*) and woolly huckleberries (*G. mosieri*).

The *Vaccinium* huckleberries, belong to the same genus as bilberries, blueberries and cranberries and their common names show the links: *V. parvifolium* are known as red huckleberries, red bilberries or red whortleberries and *V. ovatum* are called, amongst other names, evergreen huckleberries or box blueberries. Red huckleberries grow on particularly pretty plants with blue-green leaves that can, depending on the weather, turn brilliant red in autumn. The white flowers are tinged pink, blossom in late spring or early summer and then develop into coral red berries. Evergreen huckleberries are, fairly obviously (although with gardening names you can never quite tell), evergreen and have glossy black fruits. The huckleberry is the state fruit of Idaho and it is likely that it is *V. membranaceum*. This has large delicious berries, beautiful autumn colour and is particularly hardy. According to where you are in the States, it is variously called the mountain, big, tall, black, blue or thinleaf huckleberry and also the mountain or thick-leaved bilberry. This is one of those occasions when Latin names are invaluable.

These huckleberries mostly grow on large, upright shrubs ranging from 3-4 m / 10-13 ft tall and 2-3 m / 6-10 ft wide. Both *Gaylussacia* and *Vaccinium* huckleberries like well-drained soils which are acidic (pH 4.5 to 5.5) and don't dry out. Treat as you would blueberries, but expect a more interesting and unusual harvest. Both are self-fertile but you will get better crops if you grow two or more compatible plants.

Cook as for blueberries.

JAPANESE WINEBERRIES

These wonderful berries (*Rubus phoenicolasius*) are also known as wineberries or Chinese blackberries. They originated in the wilds of China and Japan and were brought to the West in the early 1900s. They belong to the extended group of hybrid berries and, along with tayberries, are the best ones to choose. They are often grown purely for their looks, but this is a mistake as the fruits are both beautiful and delicious. The graceful arching stems are covered with soft orangey-red bristles, which look particularly attractive in the winter sunshine. Little pink flowers in spring grow into small berries which change attractively from gold to red as they mature. Cleverly, the berries are encased in papery calyxes which open as the fruit ripens. They look charming and give the fruit some protection from birds. When ripe the berries pull away like raspberries. As their name implies, the berries have an interesting winey-raspberry flavour and conveniently harvest in between summer and autumn raspberries. They are self-fertile so you only need one plant. Cultivation is exactly as for blackberries. Cook as for blackberries, brambles or raspberries.

MULBERRIES

Mulberries are very special berries. Firstly, the only way to taste a mulberry is to pick one straight from the tree; they are too juicy to be transported more than a few feet – it is a good idea to wear purple when collecting them. Secondly, they grow on exquisitely beautiful trees. Thirdly, they have a splendid history (see page 27), which should justify them a place in any garden, for interest alone. As you may have gathered they are one of our favourite berries.

The main problem for many people is that they grow into large trees with an eventual height and spread of about 6 m / 20 ft or more. There are two main species of mulberry; white (*Morus alba*) and black (*M. nigra*). Unless you are planning to breed silkworms, black mulberries are the ones you want. The trees frequently lean to one side and quickly develop an aged appearance. They will eventually need to be supported by forked wooden stakes, but these simply add to the charm. They lose their leaves in winter, but even the bare branches are beautiful. They need a sunny, sheltered site and look lovely in the centre of a lawn, although they can just as well be grown as part of an orchard or in a kitchen garden. Most mulberries are self-fertile so you do not need more than one plant. They are slow-growing so you may need to wait several years for a harvest. Remember a mulberry tree will outlive you, your children and probably your children's children.

You can buy bare-rooted or container-grown plants, which should be planted in autumn. You should stake the plant for the first few years, water regularly and feed with a general fertilizer in spring. You should also mulch with well-rotted organic matter in autumn and spring; this will nourish the tree and suppress any weeds. If your tree is growing in the middle of your lawn, you should simply give a general liquid feed in spring.

Mulberries do not need pruning; simply cut away any dead or damaged branches in winter. Allow the fruits to ripen fully before harvesting; they will fall away easily when ripe. The trees are rarely troubled by pests or diseases.

Most mulberries are simply sold as the species, *Morus nigra*. 'Chelsea' is a good cultivar, with fruits that ripen early and 'King James I' bears large, well-flavoured fruits and has a pedigree dating back to the seventeenth century.

See the mulberry recipes or use in any blackberry, bramble or raspberry recipe.

GROWING BERRIES IN CONTAINERS

Most berries will grow well in containers, from alpine strawberries edging window boxes to raspberries and blueberries in larger pots. Their life spans may be slightly less than those planted in open soil, but many compact cultivars, such as the blueberry 'Top Hat' and the autumn-fruiting raspberries 'Allgold' or 'Autumn Bliss' will thrive in pots. You are never going to be self-sufficient this way, but a couple of blueberry bushes could provide you with breakfast berries for most of the summer. Two large tubs, one with a couple of blueberry bushes and cranberries beneath and the other with a wall-trained gooseberry and strawberries below would give you a respectable crop, look good and take up almost no space.

Containers are useful if you have a small garden, balcony or roof terrace and if you want to grow plants such as blueberries or cranberries, which have specific soil requirements.

You can use any container you like, but the general rule is 'the bigger the better' as most berry plants are fairly long-lived. Allow a minimum of 45-60 cm / 18-24 in for bushes and canes. Strawberries can be grown in 20 cm / 8 in pots, but they do better with more plants in a bigger container; 6 in a 60 cm / 24 in pot or 5 in a hanging basket. Sturdy wooden fruit boxes lined with plastic look particularly attractive, as do old wicker baskets, again lined with plastic. Whatever you use it must (obviously) hold compost and drain well so the plants don't become waterlogged. Lining porous containers with plastic is a good idea, as this will stop the compost drying out, but remember to make holes in the base so excess water can drain away. If possible you should put the container on feet to raise it off the ground, which will improve drainage. Remember you are trying to mimic the moisture retentive and free-draining soil of ideal beds.

You should fill the pots with a fifty-fifty mixture of a soil-based compost such as John Innes and multi-purpose, peat-free potting compost, adding up to ten per cent grit for improved drainage, if necessary. Blueberries, cranberries, bilberries and lingonberries will need ericaceous peat-free compost. This will give you a fairly heavy mixture, which will keep the pot stable and hold the nutrients without becoming compacted.

Pots will need regular watering throughout the growing season, probably on a daily basis. Cranberry and lingonberry pots should be put in saucers to collect rainwater which will maintain the necessary boggy conditions. Remember to water them (and bilberries and blueberries) with rain water rather than that from the tap as tap water is alkaline and will reduce the acidity that these plants need to survive.

Give a general fertilizer in spring and then a high potash or specialist liquid feed once a week from blossom to harvest. In spring you should also replace the top few centimetres of compost, as long as you can do this without damaging the roots. Then add a layer of mulch. Bark chips or gravel will help reduce evaporation and weeds, garden compost will also enrich the soil.

Eventually most plants will outgrow their containers. In early spring you can repot the plant into a larger container or refresh the compost in the existing one. Aim to remove twenty per cent of the old compost and any roots that are clearly pot-bound. Fill the resulting gap with fresh compost and water well.

In winter you should ensure the pots are protected from strong winds and, while they will need much less water, you shouldn't let the plants completely dry out. Plants and terracotta pots are both at risk from hard frosts. The pot can crack and the plant can suffer from drought when any water freezes solid. Wrap the pots in bubble wrap or newspaper and drape hessian or sacking round the plant when a frost is forecast.

BERRIES AS ORNAMENTALS

Many books on garden design have chapters called 'ornamental plants with berries'. How much better would be 'ornamental plants with berries you can eat'? Nearly all berries mentioned so far in this book can be grown ornamentally; honeyberries form neat bushes, Japanese wineberries are wonderful trained against a wall and mulberries quickly become venerable-looking trees but there are many more plants you can grow ornamentally which will also provide you with a crop of berries.

Berries can be grown in neat kitchen gardens or pretty potagers, but they do just as well in an ornamental garden. Unlike most vegetables, fruits can be harvested without making huge gaps in the planting scheme. Many of the fruits covered so far are very attractive, with delicate, pretty flowers and attractive jewel-like fruits. Some also have good autumn colour and striking stems in winter. Depending on the fruit they can be used to edge beds or as ground cover (alpine strawberries, cranberries and lingonberries), grown in hanging baskets (strawberries), trained along walls (gojis and all brambles, especially Japanese wineberries) or grown within hedges (gooseberries, honeyberries, brambles). They can also be grown as freestanding bushes (blueberries and honeyberries) or specimen trees (mulberries). Just beware that some can be invasive and may outgrow their allotted space.

Many other garden plants have edible berries, more or less tasty, depending on the berry. Try to have a balance between beautiful plants with interesting berries which you may not harvest that much, and plants that give you a good crop of really delicious fruit. Below is a selection of garden plants with berries you may not have thought of eating yet.

A Selection of Plants with Edible Berries

To a certain extent, the berries here and those in the foraging section on page 50-56 are interchangeable. You are quite likely to find barberries in hedges and hawthorns, rowans and elders all make delightful garden trees. Many of these berries are best used in preserves or eaten in small quantities; chokeberries for example are a great addition to a pie but we wouldn't suggest you made a crumble with them and nothing else. Not all the species have edible berries; honeyberries (*Lonicera caerulea*) are delicious, but most other *Lonicera* berries are not edible. Always check exactly which plant you intend to harvest from and avoid interplanting edible and inedible varieties. Most are self-fertile, unless otherwise mentioned.

Barberries (*Berberis* spp)
These shrubs can be evergreen or deciduous, some having beautiful

autumn colour. The yellow or orange flowers are followed by small orangy-red berries in autumn. You can buy these berries dried in Middle Eastern delicatessens, but how much better to have your own supply. *B. buxifolia* (the Magellan barberry) or *B. vulgaris* are the best, *B. thunbergii* is mildly poisonous.

Blackthorn or **Sloe** (*Prunus spinosa*)
Blackthorns form little, twisted trees with delicate spring blossom and small, blue-black fruits that ripen in late autumn. They make excellent informal hedges or can be grown as specimen trees, just beware of the thorns. The berries are too tart to eat raw but make wonderful liqueurs.

Checkerberries (*Gaultheria procumbens* syn. *G. repens*)
Also known as the partridgeberry, teaberry or wintergreen, this is a creeping, aromatic shrub, which is good for ground cover, especially in semi-shaded areas. The white or pale pink flowers which bloom in summer are followed by scarlet fruits. The oil from the berries has a minty taste and is used in toothpaste and chewing gum. It needs poor, acidic soil and is best planted beneath heath plants such as blueberries.

Chokeberries, black (*Aronia melanocarpa*), purple (*A. prunifolia*), red (*A. arbutifolia*)
The self-fertile pinky-white flowers of all chokeberries are followed by attractive autumn colour and berries the colour of the common name. The name may not sound appealing, but the tart, piney-flavoured berries are good additions to pies or made into preserves. The berries can also be used for juice; this is particularly popular in Eastern Europe where it is believed to help heart conditions.

Hackberries (*Celtis* spp.)
These are also called sugarberries and, confusingly, honeyberries. Be careful when deciding where to plant them as they can grow into large trees, eventually reaching 20 m / 70 ft. The small, sweet berries start orangy-red and ripen to deep purple or reddish-brown. The berries

have a large, hard seed, but the surrounding flesh is nice and sweet. It isn't worth picking these for cooking, but they are perfect to nibble as you walk past the tree.

Juneberries, serviceberries, shadberries, saskatoon or snowy mespilus (*Amelanchier* spp.)

In spring and early summer these trees are covered with the most exquisite white flowers. Five-petalled, they look like little stars. The young leaves are bronze-coloured and turn brilliant shades of red, yellow and purple in autumn. The berries are often sweet and juicy with nutty-tasting seeds. All juneberries are edible, but some taste better than others: *A. canadensis* (shadbush), *A.* x *grandiflora* and *A. alnifolia* (saskatoon) are good choices.

Mahonia, Oregon grapes, holly barberries (*Mahonia* spp.)

These are native to North America, but have been extensively planted elsewhere. They are hardy evergreen shrubs and have become popular garden, park and city plants; grown for their fragrant yellow spring flowers, as well as the dark purply-black fruits. One of the best is the Oregon grape (*M. aquifolium*). The leaves of mahonias look slightly like holly and the fruits like grapes, giving rise to many of the common names. The berries can be tart and are best eaten in moderate quantities. Mix them with other berries, sugar and cream or make them into jelly to accompany meat or game.

Myrtle (*Myrtus* spp.)

These grow into beautiful, aromatic shrubs, which would be worth growing anyway. In mid to late summer they produce fragrant white flowers, followed by oblong, purply-black berries. The common myrtle (*M. communis*) fruits more reliably than some others. The berries can be eaten raw, cooked, used to flavour liqueur or made into preserves, which go well with savoury dishes.

Sea buckthorn (*Hippophae rhamnoides*)

These thorny shrubs, or small trees, have attractive grey-green leaves and a bushy habit. There are tiny yellow flowers in spring which, on female plants, are followed by orange berries. You need male and female plants for a harvest of berries.

Treacleberries or false spikenard (*Maianthemum racemosum*)
This clump-forming perennial has fragrant, creamy-white flowers in spring, followed by berries which ripen from green to red in autumn. It is popular in Russia and Eastern Europe, where it is known as the Siberian pineapple. Tolerant of shade, it is an excellent ground cover plant.

BERRIES IN THE KITCHEN

It's always a good idea to follow the directions exactly the first time you try a recipe. But from then on you are on your own.

(James Beard)

General Guidelines To Using Our Recipes

Our recipes are given in both metric and imperial measurements. For best results, please follow one or the other, do not mix and match within the recipe.

Unless otherwise specified in the recipe: eggs are always large, butter is always unsalted, chocolate is minimum 70% cocoa solids, cup and spoon measurements are level.

You know your own oven best. We have found that all ovens vary and have their own idiosyncratic hot and cold spots. The best way to be sure is to use an oven thermometer rather than rely on the temperature gauge knob. In baking, use your own judgement and don't be afraid to cook for another 10 minutes or take something out of the oven a little early if it is not yet, or already, golden brown or set to the recipe instructions.

Cooking by Instinct

We are both instinctive cooks; at least that is our excuse for playing fast and loose with recipes. We use recipes as a guide and an inspiration, except when we follow them slavishly. We, and our friends and family, have tested the recipes in this book so if you follow them you should get a good result every time. However, as you gain in confidence, please feel free to adapt our recipes to your own tastes. If you don't have ginger, try chilli, if you don't like walnuts use hazelnuts, if you hate celery, leave it out. Your recipe won't be the same as ours but it might be even be better; if it is email and let us know.

What we have found over the years, is that some flavours go really well together and if you are looking to adapt recipes to what is in season, what you have in stock or what you fancy eating, you can't go far wrong if you match the following.

Berry	Herbs	Spices	Other Fruits	Meat & Fish	Other
Blackberries		Cinnamon, Ginger	Apples, Lemons, Peaches	Duck, Game, Beef	Cream, Custard, Hazelnuts, Red Wine, Goat's Cheese, Pastry
Blueberries	Lavender, Thyme	Cinnamon, Ginger,	Lemons, Limes, Pineapple	Bacon	Cream Cheese, Brown Sugar, Sour Cream, Almonds, Oats
Cranberries		Cloves, Allspice, Chilli	Apples	Ham, Poultry	Chestnuts, Walnuts
Goji Berries		Cumin		Chicken	Rice

Gooseberries		Ginger	Elderberries & Elderflowers	Mackerel & other Oily Fish, Pork	Honey, Cream
Honeyberries			Pears, Lemons		Vanilla Ice cream, Brie and other Soft Cheeses
Juniper Berries		Coriander, Black Pepper		Duck, Goose, Game, Pork, Smoked Salmon	Potatoes, Spinach
Raspberries	Mint	Vanilla, Nutmeg, Cinnamon	Mangoes, Melons, Pears, Bananas		Chocolate, Cream, Coconut, Almonds, Whisky, Rose
Strawberries	Basil, Mint, Rosemary	Black pepper, Chillies, Poppy Seeds	Watermelon, Apricots, Passionfruit, Rhubarb, Orange		Chocolate, Cream, Pistachios, Port, Balsamic Vinegar, Spinach, Meringue, Rosewater, Rum

Decorating with Berries

As well as being delicious, berries are ideal for decorating your food. We all eat with our eyes and a beautiful plate is well on the way to being an empty plate. Here are some of our favourite ideas:

Use fresh berries tumbled up on top of cakes, mousses and fools to add flavour and prettiness. A light sprinkling of icing (confectioners') sugar added just before serving will make them look even lovelier.

Should you have a cake that has sunk a bit in the middle do not despair, just fill the hollow with whipped cream and berries and pretend it was meant to be like that.

Pipe little rosettes of cream around the rim of cakes and desserts using a star nozzle and top each with a strawberry half (very fifties we know but retro is the new vintage).

Seek out raspberry or strawberry pearls. You should be able to buy them online if they are not in your local cake decorating store. These little bubbles of concentrated fruit juice encased in a thin alginate shell are really amazing. Drop a few in a champagne cocktail (very chic) or sprinkle over the surface of berry puddings or cupcakes.

Chocolate dipped strawberries are luscious. Make sure you choose very firm strawberries and allow the melted chocolate to cool a little before dipping the strawberry and balancing it on a cake rack to set. Pop the stem, if they have one, through the holes in the rack for balance or just stand the whole berry on the rack pointed end up. Place a sheet of baking parchment under the rack - that way you can peel off any little drips of chocolate once set and eat them, a cook's perk. For the most impressive chocolate dipped strawberries, dip first in white chocolate, allow to set and then dip again in dark chocolate making sure the dark layer comes only three quarters of the way up the white layer. For the ultimate in glitz and glam, a little gold leaf or gold leaf sparkles (make sure you get the edible kind) sprinkled over the dark chocolate looks fabulous.

Frosted berries add a touch of icy sophistication to cakes and desserts and are particularly apt at Christmas. The best frosted berries are made with firm fruit like blueberries, cranberries or honeyberries (haskaps). Wash and thoroughly dry the fresh berries, then, using small paint or pastry brush, brush each fruit with lightly beaten egg white and dip in bowl of caster (superfine) sugar and twirl to coat thoroughly. Leave to dry on a rack.

Adding a shiny glaze will give a really professional finish to your fruit tarts. You need a clear jelly or jam without seeds or "bits". Redcurrant, cranberry, apricot or apple all work well. Apricot or apple give shine but little flavour so are best if you are wanting your tart contents to be the key flavour. Sieve the jam if necessary to make sure it is absolutely smooth, then heat with a little water or a tablespoon of Kirsch and using a pastry brush, carefully brush over the surface of the tart.

Toffee berries taste yummy and are very attractive but they will only hold for an hour or two so need to be done quite close to serving. Again best results are from fairly firm berries: strawberries, blueberries and honeyberries (haskaps) all work well. Put half a cup of water in a heavy-bottomed pan with one cup of granulated sugar and a quarter of a cup of golden (light corn) syrup. Heat gently to dissolve the sugar completely, bring to the boil and cook until the mixture becomes a light caramel colour (or reaches 300 degrees on a sugar thermometer). Remove from the heat and wait for the bubbles to stop, then immediately dip in the fruit up to three quarters and place on waxed paper to set. Be very, very careful not to let your fingers touch the sugar mixture, which is extremely hot and will burn. For the smaller berries, it is wise to use a toothpick or skewer to dip them to avoid any danger of burnt fingers.

A berry sauce or coulis drizzled over your dessert or pooled attractively on the plate will add a welcome touch of colour and flavour to a creamy pudding and elevate bought ice cream to a serve-to-friends dessert. Just whiz the berries in a food processor, sieve if they are very seedy, taste and add a little icing (confectioners') sugar or a squirt of lemon juice to adjust the sweetness to taste.

Berried ice cubes look very summery in drinks. Half fill your ice cube trays with water and freeze, lay one or more berries on the frozen surface, top up the tray with more water to cover the berry completely and freeze. Using berry juice instead of water makes pretty coloured ice cubes.

There are few things better than fresh berries served simply with cream and at the beginning of the season this is where you will always start. Ideally collect your berries fresh from the plant (from your garden or your local pick-your-own farm) and give them a quick wash or brush and eat whilst they are still warm from the sun. If you can avoid refrigerating them do, as it does tend to dull the flavour, although obviously if you are not using them in the next couple of hours you will need to keep them in the fridge to avoid spoilage. Once you have eaten your fill of fresh berries, do try some of these recipe ideas.

BREAKFAST WITH BERRIES

BANANA BERRY SMOOTHIE

This is a delicious start to the morning and ensures you have ticked off one of your five a day before you have even finished the newspaper, resulting in a smug glow of self-satisfaction as you fight your way in to work on the tube. If you use frozen berries, the smoothie will be deliciously cold.

Serves 1

100 g / 3 ½ oz berries (raspberries, blackberries and blueberries are all good)
1 banana, sliced
5 tablespoons of yoghurt

Put everything into a blender and blitz till smooth.

BERRY GRANOLA BARS

These make a fabulous breakfast on the run or mid-morning pick-me-up. Don't fool yourself these are the diet option; they do contain a healthy dose of butter, but we have always believed that taste is more important than calorie counting and all those berries and the chia seeds make them a superfood.

The main issue with home-made granola bars is making sure they don't crumble. The best way to do this is to press down really firmly before you bake them (use an oiled spoon) and then press again when they come out the oven. We also like to give them a short second bake as this firms them up a little and means each one gets that lovely caramelised edge.

Makes 16

175 g / 6 oz / 1 ½ sticks butter
150 g / 5 oz / ½ cup clear honey
200 g / 7 oz / 1 cup demerara (raw) sugar
350 g / 12 oz / 4 cups porridge (rolled) oats
1 teaspoon ground cinnamon
85 g / 2 ½ oz pecan nuts, roughly chopped
85 g / 2 ½ oz dried blueberries or honeyberries (haskaps)
85 g / 2 ½ oz dried cranberries
85 g / 2 ½ oz goji berries
85 g / 2 ½ oz pumpkin seeds
50 g / 1 ½ oz ground almonds
50 g / 1 ½ oz chia seeds

Preheat the oven to 190 C / 375 F / Gas 5. Line the base of a 33 x 23 cm / 13 x 9 in baking tin (jelly roll pan) with baking parchment.

Melt the butter and honey in a saucepan and stir in the sugar. Cook gently over a low heat for 5 minutes, stirring until the sugar has dissolved. Bring to the boil and boil rapidly for 1-2 minutes, stirring all the time, until the mixture has thickened into a smooth caramel coloured sauce. Mix in the remaining ingredients and stir to combine.

Spoon into the tin and press down well with the back of an oiled spoon. Bake for 15 minutes until just beginning to brown around the edges. Press down again with the oiled spoon. Let cool in the tin. Run a knife around edges to loosen and turn out. Peel off the backing paper and cut into squares.

Line a baking tray (cookie sheet) with baking parchment and

place the granola squares on top and bake again for about 5 minutes at 190 C / 375 F / Gas 5. Store in an airtight tin.

Toasted Muesli

This is our standard breakfast, ideally served with spoonfuls of plain yoghurt and a few fresh berries picked fresh from the garden and dropped into the breakfast bowl.

You can tailor this to your own taste. If you prefer it nuttier or fruitier just adjust the mix. Substitute fruit and nuts according to what you like best or what you have in the cupboard.

Makes about 1kg / 2 lb

75 g / 2 ½ oz / ¼ cup clear honey (raw honey if you can get it)
60 ml / 2 fl oz / ¼ cup olive oil
45 g / 1 ½ oz soft brown sugar
500 g / 1 lb / 5 ½ cups porridge (rolled) oats
60 g / 2 oz brazil nuts
60 g / 2 oz hazelnuts
60 g / 2 oz walnuts
100 g / 3 ½ oz pumpkin seeds
100 g / 3 ½ oz linseeds
60 g / 2 oz dried blueberries
60 g / 2 oz dried strawberries (chopped)
60 g / 2 oz dried honeyberries (haskaps)

Preheat the oven to 160 C / 325 F / Gas 3. Line two baking trays (cookie sheets) with baking parchment.

Gently heat the honey, oil and sugar in a pan and simmer until the sugar has dissolved. Stir well. Put the oats, nuts and seeds into a large bowl. Pour over the honey mixture and stir well with a wooden spoon, making sure that the mixture is well-coated. Spread out evenly on the two trays.

Bake for 20-30 minutes turning the trays (cookie sheets) occasionally to make sure the mix browns evenly. If you have to place the trays on different shelves in the oven you will need to swop them round half way to ensure that they cook evenly and they may take a little longer to reach that lovely golden brown colour. When the mixture is golden brown remove and leave to cool.

Once it has cooled completely, add the dried fruit and stir well to ensure an even mix of fruit and nuts. Store in an airtight container for up to one month.

Gooseberry Brose

A little taste of Scotland at breakfast. Brose is a Highland cross between Bircher Muesli and Porridge and a delicious way to start your day. Traditionally if you add "a wee dram" (well actually, equal quantities of brose and whisky), it becomes Atholl's Brose in homage to the First Earl of Atholl who quashed a Highland rebellion in 1475 by filling the rebel leader's well with this mix, making him easy to capture (canny chaps those Scots).

Serves 1

4 tablespoons porridge (rolled) oats
150 ml / 5 fl oz / ⅔ cup single cream
250 g / 8 oz gooseberries
1 tablespoon caster (superfine) sugar
Honey to serve

Heat a dry non-stick frying pan (skillet) over a medium heat. Add the oatmeal and cook for 5-7 minutes stirring occasionally until the oatmeal is a golden brown and has a lovely toasty smell. Remove the oatmeal from the pan and place in a bowl, cover with cream and soak overnight.

Put the gooseberries and sugar in a pan with a splash of water, bring to the boil and cook gently for 3-5 minutes until the fruit is soft. Cool. Squash the fruit to a chunky purée and swirl in the cream soaked oats.

If there are any rebel leaders about, this is the point you would add the whisky, but if you are a planning a day at the office probably best just to drizzle with honey and enjoy.

Blueberry Pancakes with Bacon and Maple Syrup

At the Wilderness Music Festival, the stand serving freshly made blueberry pancakes with bacon and maple syrup always has the longest queue. If you can't be bothered waiting, or outside of festival time, you can easily make these yourself. Just put some loud morning music on the stereo and imagine you are in festival land.

Serves 4

250 g / 8 oz / 1 cup ricotta
120 g / 4 oz / 1 cup blueberries plus extra to garnish
175 ml / 6 fl oz / ¾ cup milk
4 eggs, separated
125 g / 4 oz / 1 cup plain (all-purpose) flour
1 teaspoon baking powder
a pinch of salt
50 g / 1 ½ oz / 3 tablespoons butter
8 rashers streaky bacon
Maple syrup to serve

Turn your oven on to low.

Grill (broil) or fry the bacon until crisp at the edges and keep warm while you make the pancakes.

Put the ricotta, milk and egg yolks in a bowl and mix to combine. Sift together the flour, baking powder and salt, add to the ricotta mix and stir to combine. Stir in the blueberries.

Put the egg whites into a separate bowl and whisk to stiff peaks. Fold into the ricotta batter in two batches using a metal spoon.

Melt about a tablespoon of the butter in a large heavy-bottomed frying pan (skillet). Drop in large spoonfuls of the batter. Don't overcrowd the pan. Cook over a medium heat until bubbles form on the surface of the pancakes and the underside is golden brown. Carefully flip them over and continue to cook until the pancakes are cooked through. Transfer to a plate and keep warm whilst you cook the rest of the pancakes.

Place a stack of pancakes on each plate. Top with the grilled bacon and some extra blueberries. Drizzle with maple syrup and serve.

STUFFED FRENCH TOAST

This quite simply takes French Toast to a whole new level and is our absolute favourite indulgent Sunday morning breakfast treat. It is based on a Bill Granger recipe from *Sydney Food*, a book which is definitely one of our desert island cookbooks.

Serves 2

2 slices of brioche loaf cut 4 cm (1 ½ in) thick
2 slices of good ham
1 ripe peach
1 tablespoon blueberries
a pinch of nutmeg
2 eggs
125 ml / 4 fl oz / ½ cup milk
60 ml / 2 fl oz / ¼ cup double (heavy) cream
½ teaspoon cinnamon
1 teaspoon granulated sugar
Maple syrup to serve

Peel and slice the peach.

Preheat your oven to 180C / 350 F / Gas 4.

Beat the eggs with the milk and cream, add the nutmeg and pour into a shallow bowl large enough to take the brioche slices.

With a small sharp-bladed knife carefully cut a slit in the side of each of the brioche slices to form a pocket leaving at least 1 cm / ½ in around three of the sides. Fold the ham slice around a couple of slices of peach and a few blueberries and stuff this into the pocket. Reserve any leftover peach slices and blueberries to serve.

Put the stuffed brioche into the milk and egg mix and leave to soak for a couple of minutes. Turn over and soak the other side whilst you melt the butter in a frying (sauté) pan large enough to take both slices.

When the butter is sizzling, carefully remove the brioche slices from the egg mixture and place in the pan. Cook until golden brown, turn over and cook the other side. Place on an oven tray (cookie sheet) and finish cooking in the oven for 10 minutes.

Mix the cinnamon and granulated sugar together and sprinkle on the French toast. Serve with any reserved peaches and blueberries, drizzled with maple syrup.

DESSERTS AND PUDDINGS

White Chocolate and Blueberry Terrine

This sophisticated dessert is perfect for a buffet as it can be made ahead, keeps well and slices beautifully. It is essentially jelly and cream for grown-ups, although we have found that children love it too. If you like you can make individual desserts for a dinner party. In this case use 6 120 ml / 4 fluid oz / ½ cup moulds.

We prefer gelatine leaves to powder as they give a softer set but annoyingly different brands vary in size so check the side of the packet as to the number of leaves needed to set 600 ml / 1 pint of liquid.

Serves 6

150 g / 5 oz blueberries
3 leaves of gelatine
75 ml / 2 ½ fluid oz / ⅓ cup mixed berry cordial

125 g / 4 oz good quality white chocolate
300 ml / 10 fluid oz / 1 ¼ cups double cream

Lightly oil a 600 ml / 1 pint / 2 ½ cup terrine dish
Place two gelatine leaves in a shallow dish, cover with cold water and leave to soften for 5 minutes. Mix the berry cordial with 300 ml / ½ pint / 1 ¾ cups of boiling water. Squeeze out the gelatine leaves and whisk into the cordial mix. Make sure the gelatine is completely dissolved. Pour the berry mix into the base of the terrine. Distribute the blueberries evenly along the length of the terrine and leave to cool. Put into the fridge for about an hour or until set.

Soak the remaining gelatine leaf in cold water as before. Break up the chocolate into smallish pieces and place in a small bowl, bring the cream up to boiling point and pour over the chocolate. Give it a good stir to completely melt the chocolate. Add the squeezed out gelatine leaf and stir to combine (make sure the gelatine is completely dissolved). Cool completely (but don't let it set), spoon over the set jelly and return to the fridge for a further 4 hours or overnight if preferred.

To serve dip the mould very briefly into hot water and turn out. Don't leave too long in the hot water or all that good work in setting the terrine will be wasted!

Raspberry Honeycomb Cheesecake

This is a richly indulgent dessert, definitely not for diet days but delicious, nevertheless. A decadent white chocolate cheesecake is topped with a crown of ruby raspberries and golden honeycomb, the slightly tart taste of the berries cutting the richness of the cheesecake.

You can, and indeed should, make the cheesecake the night before. The honeycomb can also be made a day or two ahead but keep it in an airtight jar or it will go gooey. Put the honeycomb on the cheesecake just before serving. If you do have leftovers, these will keep in the fridge for a few days. The honeycomb will melt into a pool of caramel but it will still taste good.

If you would like to ring the changes and use other berries, pick something tart to counter the sweetness of the honeycomb and the richness of the cheesecake; blackberries would work really well.

If you are short of time or just don't fancy making your own honeycomb, crush up 2-3 Crunchie bars and sprinkle the chocolately honeycomb crumbs in the centre of the cheesecake. It will have a little more chocolate in it, but when did a little more chocolate ever hurt a dessert?

Serves 8-10

For the honeycomb
75 g / 3 oz / ⅓ cup granulated sugar
25 g / 1 oz golden syrup (light corn syrup)
100 g / 4 oz liquid glucose
15 ml / ½ fl oz / 1 tablespoon water
15 g / ½ oz bicarbonate of soda

For the base
250 g / 8 oz hazelnut biscuits (if you can't find hazelnut biscuits use plain digestives)
125 g / 4 oz / 1 stick of butter

For the filling
200 g / 7 oz good quality white chocolate, broken into pieces
600 g / 1 lb 4 oz mascarpone
200 g / 7 oz / 1 cup caster (superfine) sugar
3 eggs
Grated zest and juice of 1 lime
300 ml / 10 fl oz / 1 ¼ cup sour cream
1 punnet of raspberries (2 if you love raspberries as much as we do)

Heat the oven to 160 C / 325 F / Gas 3.

To make the honeycomb. Line a baking tray (cookie sheet)

with baking parchment and grease with a little oil. Put the sugar, golden (light corn) syrup, liquid glucose and water into a deep heavy-bottomed pan. Heat gently to dissolve the sugar. Once you can no longer see the sugar granules turn up the heat and bring to the boil. Boil steadily for about 8-10 minutes until it turns a pale caramel colour. Watch it like a hawk, it is more forgiving than ordinary caramel due to the liquid glucose, but you don't want it to burn.

Take the pan off the heat and add the bicarbonate of soda whisking it all together with a balloon whisk. It will bubble up, fizzing alarmingly but hold your nerve and work quickly. Pour onto the prepared baking tray (cookie sheet). Leave to cool. Once cold, peel off the backing paper and break into shards, then blitz in the food processor to make a beautiful golden rubble. If you have made this ahead of time, keep in a screw top jar or airtight tin until you are ready to serve.

To make the base, line a 24 cm / 9 ½ in springform cake tin and stand it on a baking tray (cookie sheet). Blitz the biscuits in a food processor or smash in a bag to make fine crumbs. Melt the butter and mix into the biscuit crumbs and press into the base of the tin. Bake the base for 10 minutes and leave to cool on a rack.

For the filling, melt the chocolate over hot water. We find the best way to do this is to bring a large pan of water to the boil and once it is boiling turn off the heat and put the chocolate in a bain-marie or bowl over the pan and just sit it there for 5-10 minutes. Give it a stir with a spoon and it will be ready. Although the heat is turned off, the steam from the water will be enough to melt the chocolate and you don't run the risk of the chocolate ruining from being too hot.

Put the sugar and mascarpone in a large bowl and mix to combine. Add the eggs one at a time and beat until smooth. Gently fold in the lime juice and zest, the sour cream and the chocolate. Pour over the base and bake for 45 minutes to one hour. The filling should be set around the edges but still be a little wobbly in the middle. Run a knife around the edge of the cheesecake so that as it cools down and contracts it will not split in the middle. Turn off the oven and leave the cheesecake inside with the door slightly ajar (stick a wooden spoon in it) for an hour or so until it cools down a little. Take out of the oven and finish cooling completely on a rack. Cover and chill for at least two hours or overnight if you prefer.

When you are ready to serve, remove from the tin, make a ring of raspberries around the edge of the cheesecake and fill the centre with the honeycomb crumbs.

Eton Mess

A traditional dessert reputedly served at Eton College, this is quick and easy if you use shop bought meringues.

We like the kick that the addition of a drop of rum to the jam gives but if you are making this for children just leave it out. We also like to lighten the cream a little by folding in some yoghurt.

You can vary this hugely according to your whim or the available berries. Try raspberry or blackberry, perhaps using lemon curd instead of jam, or gooseberry is lovely with 2 tablespoons of elderflower cordial whipped into the cream.

Serves 8

Eton Mess

300 g / 10 oz fresh strawberries, hulled and halved (quartered if
they are really large)
50 g / 1 ½ oz meringues (about 4 nests)
250 ml / 8 fl oz / 1 cup double (heavy) cream
50 ml / 2 fl oz / ¼ cup plain full-fat yoghurt
45 ml / 1 ½ fl oz / 3 tablespoons strawberry jam (ideally home-
made see page 196)
15 ml / ½ fl oz / 1 tablespoon dark rum (optional)

Stir the rum into the jam if using. Whip the cream to soft peaks.
Don't overwhip as you will mix it some more when you are adding
the extra ingredients. Fold in the yoghurt. Stir through the jam mix
and the strawberries, to achieve a rippled effect. Break the meringues
into bite-size pieces and add to the cream mix. Stir to evenly combine.
Pile into pretty glasses or bowls and serve.

BERRY MERINGUE ROULADE

This probably the dessert we make the most often. It's reliable,
inexpensive and everyone loves it. We stole the recipe from Books for
Cooks when we worked there (they didn't mind). Your only concern
is finding a use for the egg yolks you have left over. The mulberry
apple ice cream on page 131 is the obvious answer.

You can stick to a single berry as your filling or go completely
berry-tastic and put in a wild mixture.

Serves 6-8

6 egg whites
1 pinch of salt
375 g / 12 oz / 1 ½ cups caster (superfine) sugar
250 ml / 8 fl oz / 1 cup double (heavy) cream
250 g / 8 oz berries (raspberries, strawberries, blackberries,
honeyberries (haskaps), blueberries or a mixture)

Heat the oven to 180 C / 350 F / Gas 4. Line a 33 x 23 cm / 13 x 9 in Swiss roll tin (jelly roll pan) with baking paper making sure the paper stands up 2.5 cm / 1 in taller than the tin.

Whisk the egg whites with a pinch of salt until they stand in soft drooping peaks. Gradually whisk in the sugar a tablespoon at a time until the mixture is thick and glossy. Spread the meringue mix into the lined tin and bake for 20-25 minutes until the meringue is golden and firm to the touch. Cool in the tin on a wire rack.

Lay out a piece of baking paper a little larger than your tin and invert your tin of meringue onto it. Remove the tin and the lining paper.

Whip the cream until it holds its shape and spread over the meringue. Sprinkle the berries evenly over the cream. Using the paper to guide you, roll it up from the long side to form a log of meringue, berries and cream.

ROTE GRUTZE

This traditional German dessert hails originally from Schlieswig-Holstein. Its sweet-tart berry flavour makes it a popular and refreshing summer pudding. We prefer to use crème frâiche or whipped cream cut with yoghurt for the topping, to make this a little lighter, but for the truly Teutonic experience it should be Shlagsahne (whipped cream) every time. Guten Appetit !

Serves 6

500 g / 1 lb / 3 cups fresh red or blackcurrants
500 g / 1 lb / 3 cups mixed strawberries, raspberries and blackberries
280 g / 10 oz / 1 ¼ cups golden caster (superfine) sugar
¼ cup rose wine
¼ tsp salt
2 tablespoons cornflour (cornstarch)
crème frâiche or whipped cream and extra berries to decorate

Put the currants, sugar, wine and salt in a saucepan and heat gently stirring to dissolve the sugar. Bring to the boil and simmer a few minutes until the fruit is soft.

Purée in a blender until smooth. Return to the saucepan and bring back to the boil. Mix the cornflour (cornstarch) with ¼ cup of water and stir into the purée, cook gently for five minutes until slightly thickened. Stir in the berries and remove from the heat.

Pour into 6 small glasses and chill for 2 hours or until set, overnight is fine. Top with whipped cream and a few berries to decorate.

RED FRUIT SALAD

Simple things like keeping a close colour palette add a touch of sophistication to a fruit salad.

We haven't given quantities for the fruit here as this can be scaled up or down at will and the fruit ratios switched according to the season, your preference or the number of people you are feeding.

Sugar syrup
1 cup caster (superfine) sugar
1 cup water
watermelon
strawberries
raspberries
red plums
red grapes
mint, julienned

Gradually heat the sugar and water stirring to dissolve the sugar. Boil for 3 minutes and leave to cool.

Take the rind and seeds off the watermelon and cut into bite sized chunks. Halve the strawberries and red grapes. Stone the plums and halve or quarter them depending on their size. Put all the fruit in a large serving bowl and mix gently to combine.

Pour over the cooled sugar syrup and sprinkle with a little julienned mint.

CRANACHAN

Jane's family hails from north of the border, Jane McMorland Hunter of Hafton, and so this traditional Scottish dessert is truly part of her heritage. It is simplicity itself, but like all simple dishes, it is absolutely delicious providing you use top quality ingredients, so don't skimp.

Traditionally you mix the sugar in with the toasted oatmeal but we prefer to sprinkle it with sugar before toasting as this gives the oatmeal itself a lovely caramelized taste.

Serves 4-6

60 g / 2 oz medium grade oatmeal
15 g / ½ oz / 2 tablespoons soft brown sugar
300 g / 5 oz raspberries
600 ml / 1 pint / 2 ½ cups double (heavy) cream
4 tablespoons honey
4 tablespoons whisky

Lay the oatmeal out on a lightly oiled baking tray (baking sheet) and sprinkle with the brown sugar. Put under the grill and toast until golden (watch this like a hawk, you don't want it to burn and it doesn't take long- two tweets and you are toast). Stir it around half way to make sure it browns on both sides.

Blend 100 g / 3 ½ oz of the raspberries with the whisky and honey until smooth.

Whip the cream to soft peaks. Carefully fold in two thirds of the raspberry purée to give a ripple effect.

Layer up the remaining raspberries, the toasted oatmeal and the cream mixture in serving glasses (whisky tumblers are about the right size and seem very appropriate somehow) sprinkling the top with the reserved oatmeal and drizzling with the last of the purée.

Bramble Steamed Puddings

In truth these lovely steamed puds can be made with any berry jam you have to hand: mulberry, blackberry, raspberry, strawberry all are equally delicious. If you feel like making this exotic, use the strawberry and rose jam on page 191 and add a scant ½ teaspoon of ground cardamom to the sponge mix.

Serve with thick (heavy) cream or vanilla custard for the perfect comfort pudding.

Makes 6 puddings, each one 9 x 6 cm / 3 ½ x 2 ½ in

100 g / 3 ½ oz / 7 tablespoons unsalted butter
9 tablespoons of your favourite berry jam
3 large eggs
zest of one lemon
125 g / 4 oz / ⅔ cup caster (superfine) sugar
100 g / 3 ½ oz / ¾ cup plain (all purpose) flour

Put a large pot of water with a steamer tray on to boil. Butter and flour 6 individual 250 ml / 8 fl oz / 1 cup pudding moulds. Place 1 ½ tablespoons of jam in the bottom of each mould.

Melt the butter over a low heat. Whisk the eggs, lemon zest and sugar together until light and moussey. Fold in the flour. Fold in the melted butter.

Pour into the moulds making sure they are not more than three-quarters full. Cover tightly with foil and place on the steamer rack. Place the steamer over the boiling water, put on the lid and steam for 30 minutes. Check that the water does not boil dry.

When the puddings are ready they will have risen to the top of the pudding basins and the top may even have domed up a little. Leave to rest for 5 minutes and then invert onto the serving plates and serve in a puddle of cream or custard

Simple Strawberry Ice Cream

We think of this as simple ice cream because you just whisk the sugar into the milk avoiding the stress of making a custard base. You need to use full-fat milk and cream here, as the light versions will not thicken properly.

You also absolutely must dice the strawberries to go into the ice cream very finely (about the size of chocolate chips). Remember they will be frozen and large pieces are hard on the teeth!

It goes without saying that strawberries are a starting point - any berries will do here. Pick your favourites.

Makes 1 litre / 1 ¾ pints / 4 cups

300 g / 10 oz strawberries
1 tablespoon lemon juice
150 g / 5 oz / ¾ cup granulated sugar
160 ml / 5 ½ fl oz / ⅔ cup milk
300 ml / 10 fl oz / 1 ¼ cup double (heavy) cream
1 teaspoon vanilla extract

Slice half the strawberries and add the lemon juice and 60 g/ 2 oz of the sugar and leave to sit in the fridge for a couple of hours to release the juices. Finely dice the remaining strawberries.

Take the macerated strawberries out of the fridge and whiz to a purée. Whisk the remaining sugar into the milk vigorously until it has dissolved. Add the cream, strawberry purée and vanilla extract and stir to combine.

Ideally freeze in an ice cream maker following the manufacturer's directions. If you don't have an ice cream maker, place in a lidded container in the freezer for an hour, take out and beat enthusiastically. Return to the freezer and repeat, freezing and beating, until frozen to the desired consistency.

5 minutes before the ice cream is ready, stir in the remaining diced strawberries.

If you have an ice cream maker then this is a fall-back pudding to make from store-cupboard ingredients. Choose a fairly runny jam or give the jam a quick whizz with a stick blender as any large fruit pieces will freeze like bullets and be difficult to eat.

Makes 1 litre / 1 ¾ pints / 4 cups

150 g / 5 oz / ¾ cup caster (superfine) sugar
750 g / 1 ⅔ lbs / 3 cups full-fat yoghurt
1 teaspoon vanilla essence (extract)
3-4 tablespoons of your favourite berry jam

Beat the vanilla extract, sugar and yoghurt to thoroughly combine. Churn in an ice cream maker according to the manufacturer's instructions. When nearly frozen transfer to a freezer container, swirl through the jam and freeze for an hour to set completely.

APPLE AND MULBERRY RIPPLE ICE CREAM

Unlike the previous recipes, this ice cream has a custard base. It is a little more nerve-wracking, making sure your custard thickens and doesn't curdle, but be patient and don't turn the heat up too high and you will be rewarded with lusciously rich ice cream. If you can't find any mulberries, use blackberries, and the ice cream will be just as good.

Makes 600 ml / 1 pint ice cream

250 g / 9 oz mulberries
1 large Bramley (cooking) apple
175 g / 6 oz / 1 cup sugar
300 ml / 10 fl oz / 1 ¼ cups double (heavy) cream
300 ml / 10 fl oz / 1 ¼ cups milk
½ vanilla pod, cut in half lengthways and seeds scraped out or

1 teaspoon vanilla essence (extract)
6 egg yolks

Put the mulberries and 15 g / ½ oz of the sugar and a tablespoon of cold water in a pan and heat for five minutes, or until the berries have softened. Set aside to cool.

Peel, seed and chop the apple and place in a separate pan with a tablespoon of cold water. Cook gently until the apple looses its shape and becomes a soft purée.

Pour the cream and milk into a saucepan. Add the vanilla seeds and stir well. Heat very gently to just below boiling point but do not boil.

In a separate bowl, beat the egg yolks and the remaining sugar until fluffy. Add the warm cream and milk mixture and stir well. Return the custard mixture to the saucepan used to heat the cream and continue to cook over a low heat, stirring all the time, until the mixture is thick enough to coat the back of a spoon.

Drain the berries through a sieve (strainer), set over a bowl and reserve the liquid. Place the sieve (strainer) over another bowl and push the berries through the sieve to form a purée, add a little of the reserved liquid if the purée is very thick and set aside.

Add the apple purée to the custard mix. Transfer to an ice cream maker and churn according to manufacturer's instructions. If you don't have an ice cream maker, use the method in the simple strawberry ice cream recipe. Ten minutes before the end of the churning, add the berry purée so it stirs through in a ripple effect.

Gooseberry Fool

Any berry fruit can be made a fool of, as they say. Just cook the berries down to a purée and swirl through equal quantities of whipped cream and yoghurt.

We like tart fruits to get a contrast between fruit and cream and so tend to go for gooseberry, raspberry or blackberry but do try other berries as the whim takes you. You can throw in little touches of sophistication: a tablespoon of elderflower cordial cooked with the gooseberries, some chopped crystallized ginger folded through blackberries, a shot of rose water in a strawberry fool, but to be honest, the simple classic is so good we just come back to that every time. If you can get pink gooseberries these are particularly pretty.

Serves 4

250 g / 8 oz gooseberries, topped and tailed
3 tablespoons caster (superfine) sugar
200 ml / 7 fl oz / ¾ cup thick Greek yoghurt
200 ml / 7 fl oz / ¾ cup double (heavy) cream

Put the gooseberries into a saucepan with the sugar and a splash of water and cook until the fruit collapses, around 10 minutes. Mash or whizz to a chunky purée and set aside to cool completely.

Whip the cream to soft peaks and gently fold in the yoghurt. Swirl the gooseberry purée through to give a ripple effect and pile into pretty glasses. Serve chilled.

APPLE AND BLACKBERRY PIE OR CRUMBLE

We use this really versatile filling recipe for both pies and crumbles and can never quite decide which we prefer: a melting shortcrust with a little sugar crunch or a nutty crumble. Try both and see which is your favourite.

You can switch round the fruits a little if you like – a pear and raspberry combination is delicious, or give it a more autumnal feel by using sloe gin instead of the apple brandy.

Serves 4-6

Filling
1 large Bramley (cooking) apple
3 medium sized dessert apples

150 g / 5 oz blackberries
1 tablespoon of Calvados or apple brandy (optional)
60 g / 2 oz / ⅓ cup dark brown sugar
a squeeze of lemon juice

Piecrust
500 g / 1 lb / 4 cups plain (all-purpose) flour
1 good pinch of salt
250 g / 8 oz / 2 sticks of very cold butter, cubed
2 egg yolks
1-2 tablespoons of cold water
1 tablespoon demerara (raw sugar)
1 tablespoon of milk

Crumble
100 g / 3 ½ oz / 7 tablespoons unsalted butter
100 g / 3 ½ oz / 4/5 cup plain (all purpose) flour
60 g / 2 oz / ⅓ cup demerara (raw) sugar
75 g / 2 ½ oz / ¾ cup rolled (porridge) oats
75 g / 2 ½ oz hazelnuts, chopped

To make the filling, peel and core both types of apple and cut
them into chunks and add a squeeze of lemon juice to stop them
discolouring. Put the apple in a large heavy-bottomed saucepan
over a medium heat with the brown sugar and the Calvados or
apple brandy, if using. If you are not using the brandy, then add a
tablespoon of water. Cover with a lid, bring up to a gentle simmer
and let it stew for 5 minutes or so until the Bramley (cooking) apple
has softened and started to break down. Remove the lid and cook for
another 5 minutes. Taste for sweetness, since apples vary in sweetness
and it is best to adjust the sugar to taste. Stir in the blackberries
and remove from the heat. If you are using this for a pie, let the
filling cool completely before adding to the pastry case. If you are in
crumble mode, you can sprinkle on the crumble immediately and
pop it into the oven.

For a pie, preheat the oven to 200 C / 400 F / Gas 6. Put the flour and salt into a food processor and pulse a couple of times. Add the cubed butter and process until the mixture resembles fine breadcrumbs. If you don't have a food processor just rub the butter into the flour and salt using your fingertips. Add the egg yolks and pulse or mix till just combined. If it is too dry just add a tablespoon of cold water. Turn out onto a floured surface and knead briefly to make a flat round. Wrap in cling film (saran wrap) and place in the fridge to rest for half an hour.

Roll out the pastry and use two thirds to line a 24 cm / 9 in metal or ceramic pie dish. Fill with the apple and berry filling and roll out the final third to make the pie top. Cut a small slit in the centre of the top to allow steam to escape and brush with a tablespoon of milk to glaze. Put into the oven and cook for 20 minutes. Turn down the heat and cook a further 20 minutes until the top is golden. Serve with cream or custard.

For the crumble, set the oven to 180 C / 350 F / Gas 4. Whiz the butter, sugar and flour together in a food processor to make fine crumbs or rub in with your fingertips. Stir in the rolled oats and chopped hazelnuts. Put the apple berry filling into a pretty china pie dish and sprinkle the crumble topping thickly over the top. Bake for 20 minutes or until the top is golden and the filling is gently bubbling round the edges.

Strawberry Mousse Cake

This is a visually stunning dessert from Alice Medrich's book *Chocolat* which will have your guests wondering "how did she do that"? None of the individual components are difficult, but it does take a bit of time, so make it a day ahead and keep in the fridge.

The sponge mix makes more than you need, but just wrap the other half well in cling film (saran wrap) and freeze ready for next time or for an impromptu trifle. Admit it, we all want a lifestyle that allows for impromptu trifle.

Serves 10

For the sponge layer
60 ml / 2 fl oz / ¼ cup milk
30 g / 1 oz / 2 tablespoons butter
75 g / 2 ½ oz / ¾ cup plain (all purpose) flour
1 teaspoon baking powder
150 g / 5 oz / ¾ cup caster (superfine) sugar
3 eggs
3 egg yolks

For the mousse layer
275 g / 9 oz white chocolate, chopped
350 ml / 12 fl oz / 1 ½ cups double (heavy) cream
3 tablespoons Kirsch

To assemble
400 g / 14 oz / 1 large punnet of strawberries
60 ml / 2 fl oz / ¼ cup apricot jam (use a smooth jam with no bits)
2 tablespoons pistachio nuts, finely chopped

Preheat the oven to 200 C / 400 F / Gas 6. Line the bottom of a 20 cm / 8 in springform cake tin with baking parchment.

Heat the milk and butter in a small pan over a medium heat until the butter melts. Keep hot but do not simmer.

Sift the flour with the baking powder. Put the sugar, eggs and yolks in a large heatproof bowl and whisk until light and fluffy. Place the bowl over a pan of simmering water and, whisking occasionally, heat it to lukewarm. Check by putting a (clean) finger in it, it should be blood heat. Once the mixture is lukewarm, remove from the heat and whisk vigorously (an electric mixer is best) until it has cooled and tripled in volume. It will look a little like a pale yellow whipped cream.

Gently fold in one third of the flour mixture using a rubber spatula. Repeat twice to incorporate all the flour. Pour in the hot milk and butter and fold well until you can no longer see traces of bright yellow liquid. Pour into the prepared cake tin and bake 20-30 minutes until golden brown and starting to shrink slightly from the edges of the tin. Cool in the tin on a wire rack.

Once completely cool, remove from the tin. Cut the sponge in half horizontally through the centre so you have two identical round sponges. Wrap and freeze one half for use another day. Put one half back into the original tin (or in a dessert ring if you have such a thing).

Take about 10 strawberries of approximately the same height. Hull them and cut in half vertically and arrange them pointed ends up around the outside of the tin with the cut sides fitting close against the sides of the tin. You should have a ring of half strawberries now all around the edge of the tin. Fill in the middle with whole berries (pointed ends up).

Now make the mousse layer. Put the chocolate and the Kirsch in a heatproof bowl. Bring a saucepan of water to the boil, remove from the heat and place the bowl of chocolate over the water to melt. Stir occasionally until melted and smooth. Let cool until room temperature but not set.

Whisk the double (heavy) cream to soft peaks. Gently fold in the white chocolate mix. Immediately pile the mousse over the berries in the tin, pushing down gently to ensure the mousse gets down between the berries. You can pipe it but we have found a firm hand with the spatula is sufficient. Smooth the top. Place in the refrigerator for at least 4 hours to set.

Remove the springform outside of the tin to unmould your dessert onto a serving plate. Put the apricot jam into a small pan and gently warm to create a brushable glaze. Carefully brush the outside edge of the sponge with melted apricot jam and pat on chopped pistachios.

Boysenberry Clafoutis

Clafoutis are traditionally made with cherries but big fat juicy berries nestling in a clafoutis batter are even more delicious. We have made blackberry, boysenberry, blueberry and raspberry clafoutis, all to popular acclaim.

It's a handy hot dessert to have in your repertoire as you can make the batter up to 24 hours ahead. Indeed, it is all better for standing for a bit. Just keep it in the fridge. Then all you just need to do is strew a dish with berries, pour over the batter and pop it into the oven as you serve the main course. Make this in a pretty dish you can take to the table as it is quite messy to serve.

It is totally fine to use frozen, or even, perish the thought, tinned (canned) berries in a clafoutis.

Serves 4-6

50 g / 2 oz / ½ stick butter
4 eggs
125 g / 4 oz / ⅔ cup caster (superfine) sugar
50 g / 2 oz / ½ cup plain (all purpose) flour
250 ml / 8 fl oz / 1 cup whole milk
1 teaspoon vanilla extract
450 g / 1 lb boysenberries
Icing (confectioners') sugar to drench

Preheat your oven to 190 C / 375 F / Gas 5. Melt the butter in a small pan or the microwave.

Whisk the eggs together in a large bowl using an electric beater as this will give you a better batter than a food processor. Add the sugar, and then the flour, and then the melted butter, and finally the milk and vanilla extract, whisking well after each addition. Set aside to rest for at least 20 minutes.

Lightly butter a 23 cm / 9 in dish. The base needs to be completely flat. Spread the boysenberries over the base of the dish and pour in the batter. Place in the oven and bake for about 40 minutes until puffed and golden brown. Sprinkle with icing (confectioners') sugar and serve immediately with thick cream.

You can use any mixture of berries here for your filling although ideally you want a few tart berries in the mix. We favour a roughly equal mix of raspberries, strawberries, cherries and blueberries. Raspberries are best for the soaking syrup.

We like to make little individual puddings for a pretty plated dessert but you can use a single large pudding dish and serve in slices if you prefer.

Makes 8 x 250 ml / 8 oz / 1 cup individual puddings

Sugar syrup
75 g / 2 ½ oz / ⅓ cup caster (superfine) sugar
150 ml / 5 fl oz / ⅔ cup water
500 g / 1 lb mixed berries (hull, halve or quarter strawberries, pit and halve cherries)

For the purée
250 g / 8 oz raspberries
25 g / 1 oz / ¼ cup icing (confectioners') sugar

1 loaf good white bread, thinly sliced

To make the sugar syrup, bring the sugar and water to the boil, stirring to dissolve the sugar. Boil for 3-5 minutes. Add the mixed berries and remove from the heat and leave to cool. Drain, reserving the liquid.

Whizz the raspberries and icing (confectioners') sugar together to make a purée. Add to the juices from the drained berries.

Cut 8 circles from the slices of bread to fit the bottom of your moulds. Dip the slices in the raspberry syrup. Don't leave to soak, you don't want them to disintegrate, and place one in the bottom of each mould. Cut oblong pieces from the bread, dip and use to line the sides of the moulds. Fill the centre with the drained berries. Cut

8 more circles to fit the top of the mould, dip them in syrup and place on top of the moulds enclosing the puddings. If you have any leftover syrup keep this to drizzle over the puddings when you serve.

Cover with cling film (saran wrap), place a weight on top of each one and put in the fridge for 3-4 hours or overnight.

When you are ready to serve, remove the film, run a flat knife round the edge of the pudding moulds and turn out. Serve with cream.

Iced Berries with White Chocolate

This is the signature dessert at The Ivy, a well-known London restaurant and the haunt of the glitterati. It is simplicity itself to make and ideal for unexpected guests as it requires no advance preparation. Just keep some frozen berries in the freezer and a bar of white chocolate to hand. Of course, Jane says it is impossible to keep white chocolate.

Good quality white chocolate is essential here, the cheap stuff can taste over sweet and sickly.

Serves 8

1 kg / 2 lb frozen mixed berries
600 g / 1 lb 5 oz good quality white chocolate
600 ml / 1 pint / 2 ½ cups double (heavy) cream

Break the chocolate up into small pieces and place it and the cream into a bain-marie or heat-proof bowl. Bring a pot of water to the boil, remove from the heat and place the bain-marie over the water and let the cream heat through and the chocolate melt, stirring every so often.

Five minutes before serving divide the berries between the individual dessert plates and leave at room temperature to take the chill off. Transfer the hot chocolate sauce to a serving jug.

Place the berries in front of your guests and pour over the hot chocolate sauce.

Berries

Gooseberry Curd Cheesecake

This layered cheesecake is a lovely way to use berry curd (see page 200). We like to top it with a ginger gooseberry compote which picks up the ginger notes in the base and adds a refreshing tartness to cut through the richness of the cheesecake.

Serves 8

For the base
250 g / 8 oz gingernut biscuits (ginger cookies)
75 g / 2 ½ oz / 5 tablespoons butter

For the filling
360 g / 12 oz cream cheese
1 tablespoon plain (all purpose) flour
zest and juice of half a lemon
2 large eggs
150 ml / 5 fl oz / ½ cup sour cream

For the topping
200 g / 7 oz gooseberry curd
1 large egg

For the compote
350 g gooseberries
25 g / 1 oz / ¼ cup caster (superfine) sugar
3 tablespoons ginger cordial

Whizz the biscuits (cookies) in a food processor or put into a bag and bash with a rolling pin to form fine crumbs. Melt the butter and mix in the crumbs. Press into the base and sides of a 20 cm / 8 in springform pan lined with baking parchment. Put in the fridge for at least 30 minutes to firm up. Preheat your oven to 160 C / 325 F / Gas 3.

Beat the cream cheese for a couple of minutes, add in the flour, lemon juice and zest, and eggs and beat well to combine. Stir in the sour cream and pour into the gingernut crust. Place the tin on a baking tray (sheet) in case of any leakage and bake for 40 minutes.

Beat the egg into the curd and spread over the top of the partially cooked cheesecake. Return to the oven and bake for another 40 minutes or until the cheesecake is cooked. It will be firm at the edges but still a little wobbly in the middle. Turn off the oven and leave the cheesecake to cool in the oven but with the door slightly ajar (pop a wooden spoon in it). Remove from the oven, refrigerate and chill overnight.

Put the gooseberries, sugar and ginger cordial in a pan and cook gently over a low heat for 5 minutes or until the fruit is soft but still retains some shape. Cool.

To serve, unmould the cheesecake onto a plate and top with the compote.

Lemon and Blackberry Crunch

In the 1990s, Xanthe Clay began a column in *The Daily Telegraph* where readers wrote in with recipe for seasonal gluts: gooseberries, raspberries and the like. The best recipes were then published in *It's Raining Plums*, which is one of the most useful seasonal cookbooks. This recipe was originally sent in by Chris and Jill James of Abergele in Wales and if they are reading this, we would like to say 'Thank you' for this idea.

The quantities can be adjusted, as you wish; as long as you have sufficient butter to just hold the biscuits together, none of the quantities matter. You can make it more or less lemony, or more or less fruity, or play about with the balance of the layers.

This pudding tends to fall apart when served; make it in a glass bowl so it arrives at the table showing its pretty layers as they will be lost when you serve it.

Serves 6

300 g / 10 oz / 1 packet of ginger biscuits (cookies)
175 g / 6 oz / 1 ½ sticks butter, melted
500 ml / 18 fl oz / 1¾ cups crème fraîche (half fat if you are
making an attempt to be virtuous)
½ jar home-made or good quality lemon curd
500 g / 1 lb blackberries

Crush the biscuits until they resemble breadcrumbs. The easiest way to do this is in a food processor or put them in a plastic bag and then bash with a rolling pin. Put the crumbs into a bowl and pour the melted butter over, mixing well.

Fold the crème fraîche and lemon curd gently together.

In a large glass bowl spread a layer of the biscuit crumbs followed by a layer of lemony cream and then a layer of blackberries. Don't flatten the base layer; you want a loose, crumbly texture. Continue the layers, finishing with a layer of fruit. Sprinkle with icing sugar if the berries are very tart.

Put into the fridge and, ideally eat within a couple of hours. Any leftovers are delicious the next day, but the layers will merge and the pudding won't look so attractive.

HEART ATTACK PUDDING

This is based on a recipe in *The French Kitchen*, by Joanne Harris and Fran Warde. They call it a cheesecake, but it is so rich that we feel ours is perhaps a better title. Our version includes raspberries, which give a fresh contrast to the chocolate.

Serves 6

200 g / 7 oz chocolate chip cookies
100 g / 3 ½ oz / 7 tablespoons butter
150 g / 5 ½ oz / 1 cup white chocolate

70 g / 2 ½ oz / ½ cup dark chocolate
225 ml / 8 fl oz / 1 cup crème fraîche
75 g / 2 ¾ oz / ⅓ cup demerara (raw) sugar
225 ml / 8 fl oz / 1 cup double (heavy) cream
200 g / 7 oz / 1½ cups raspberries

Crush the cookies until they resemble breadcrumbs. The easiest way to do this is to either whiz them in a food processor or put them in a plastic bag and bash with a rolling pin. Put the crumbs into a bowl, melt the butter and pour over, mixing well. Lightly grease a 23 cm / 9 in loose-bottomed tart tin and line the base with baking parchment. Pour the mixture into the tin and push down so it is flat. Put in the fridge to cool and set firm.

Grate the white chocolate.

Bring a large pan of water to the boil, break the dark chocolate into pieces and put in a bowl which will fit inside the pan. Put the bowl into the boiling water, ensuring that the water does not bubble over the rim. Once the chocolate has melted, remove from the heat.

Beat together the crème fraîche and demerara (raw) sugar till blended. Then add the double (heavy) cream and mix well. Divide the mixture into two bowls, putting roughly ⅔ in one bowl and ⅓ in the other. The exact quantities don't matter; you just want more of what will be the white chocolate mixture so the filling doesn't become too dark. Add the melted dark chocolate to the smaller quantity and mix in. Add the grated white chocolate to the larger quantity and stir through.

Dollop the two chocolate mixtures randomly onto the biscuit base. Swirl gently with a knife; be careful not to completely blend the two mixtures. Arrange the raspberries on the top. Chill for 3 hours before serving.

Raspberry Truffles

These are the perfect sweetmeat to serve after dinner with coffee when you think really can't eat another thing but fancy a little something sweet.

If you are more of a strawberry girl than a raspberry lover, use white chocolate and freeze dried strawberry crumbs and swop the rum for brandy or even strawberry liqueur if you have any lurking at the back of a cupboard.

Makes 20

100 ml / 3 fl oz / ½ cup double (heavy) cream
200 g / 7 oz good quality dark chocolate, broken into small pieces
35 g / 1 ¼ oz / 2 tablespoons unsalted butter, cubed
1 tablespoon dark rum
4 tablespoons freeze-dried raspberry crumbs
unsweetened cocoa powder, sifted, for coating

Place the cream in a small heavy-bottomed saucepan and bring up to boiling point. Remove from the heat, add the chocolate and stir until the chocolate has melted. Add in the cubed butter and stir again until melted and combined. Add the rum and raspberry crumbs and stir again. Leave to cool and refrigerate for a couple of hours or overnight until the mixture is firm enough to roll into balls.

Working quickly, roll teaspoons of the mixture into balls (or if you have a melon baller, this is useful here) and roll in the cocoa. Return to the fridge to store.

For the best flavour take out of the fridge a half hour or so before serving to return to room temperature, although the odd one sneaked straight from the fridge tastes pretty good too.

TARTE AUX MYRTILLES

Myrtilles are often translated as 'blueberries', but they are actually bilberries, which are smaller, more intensely flavoured and, unless you live near a local source, much harder to come by. If you can't find any use blueberries, honeyberries or bottled bilberries.

Serves 4

Pâte sucrée
100 g / 3 ½ oz / ¾ cup plain flour
50 g / 2 oz / 4 tablespoons butter
50 g / 2 oz / ¼ cup caster (superfine) sugar
2 egg yolks

Crème pâtissière
300 ml / 10 fl oz / 1 ½ cups milk
1 vanilla pod, split
2 eggs
50 g / 2 oz / ¼ cup caster (superfine) sugar
25 g / 1 oz / 1/5 cup plain flour

Topping
250-300 g / 9-10 oz / 1 ½ -2 cups bilberries or blueberries,
depending on the thickness of fruit you want
Redcurrant jelly to glaze (you won't need this if using bottled
fruit)

To make the pâte sucrée, sift the flour into a bowl and rub in the
butter, using your fingertips until the mixture resembles breadcrumbs.
Mix in the sugar and then add the egg yolks, kneading to form a
dough. You may need to add a little water, but be careful not to make
the dough too soft. Wrap in cling film (saran wrap) and put in the
fridge for at least 30 minutes.

Preheat the oven to 180 C / 350 F / Gas 4. Grease a 20 cm / 8
in loose-bottomed tart tin. Roll out the pastry on a lightly floured
surface and line the tin. The pastry will probably break up, but don't
worry, just patch any gaps with offcuts. The base won't show and the
edges look better with a slightly rustic appearance; just make sure the
sides are sufficiently tall and firm to hold the crème pâtissière. Line the
pastry case with greaseproof paper and fill with baking beans. Bake
for 10 minutes, remove the beans and paper and bake for another 5-10

minutes to dry the pastry.

To make the crème pâtissière, pour the milk into a pan, add the vanilla pod and bring just to the boil. Remove from the heat and leave for ten minutes to infuse. Strain and discard the vanilla pod. Put the eggs, sugar and flour into a bowl and beat together. Add the milk, a little at a time, stirring well. Pour back into the pan and return to the heat. Stir all the time as the mixture thickens. Once it is the consistency of thick custard, pour the mixture into a clean bowl, through a sieve (strainer) if there are any lumps. Cover the surface with cling film (saran wrap) to prevent a skin forming and leave to cool.

When the pastry and custard are both cold, pour the custard into the tart and spread evenly.

To glaze the fruit, put the redcurrant jelly in a pan and heat gently till melted. Add a little water as necessary; you want a very runny consistency. Remove from the heat, allow to cool slightly and then add the berries into the pan. Gently stir till they are all coated with the jelly. Using a slotted spoon, spread the berries in an even layer on top of the crème pâtissière.

Put into the fridge and serve cold. The crème pâtissière and pastry case can both be made a day ahead (put the crème pâtissière in the fridge until you need it), but, ideally don't assemble the tarte more than a couple of hours before you are going to eat it.

Strawberry Tiramisu

Based on a recipe from Leiths Cooking School, this is tiramisu for those who don't like coffee, or fancy a change. It takes the fundamentals of tiramisu: the soaked sponge fingers, the mascarpone and the booze but uses strawberries to make it fruitier and lighter. Try it, we promise you'll love it as much as the original. You need to make this the night before, so the flavours have a chance to mingle.

Do note, this dessert contains uncooked eggs so do not serve to expectant mothers or those with compromised immune systems.

Serves 6

340 g / 12 oz mascarpone cheese
2 tablespoons single cream
85 g / 3 oz / ⅓ cup plus 1 tablespoon caster (superfine) sugar
1 teaspoon vanilla extract
2 eggs, separated
85 ml / 3 fluid oz / ⅓ cup rum
85 ml / 3 fl oz / ⅓ cup milk
255 g / 9 oz sponge finger biscuits
450 g / 1 lb strawberries, hulled
150 ml / 5 fl oz / ⅔ cup double (heavy) cream
4 amaretti biscuits, crushed

Beat the mascarpone with the single cream, sugar, vanilla extract and egg yolks.

In a separate clean bowl whisk the egg whites to stiff peaks and fold them into the mascarpone mixture.

Mix the rum with the milk in a shallow dish. Dip a third of the sponge fingers in the mix one at a time and use to line the base of a shallow serving dish. Cover with half the marscapone mix. Slice half the strawberries and layer onto the mascarpone.

Dip another third of the biscuits into the rum and milk and layer these on top of the strawberries. Top with the remaining mascarpone.

Dip the last of the sponge fingers and lay these on top. Whip the double (heavy) cream to soft peaks and pile on top of the sponge fingers. Halve the remaining strawberries and decorate the top with these and the crushed amaretti biscuits. Place in the fridge overnight.

Coconut Pannacotta with Spiced Berry Compote

A soft wobbly pannacotta is a beautiful thing and perfectly offset by a lightly spiced berry compote. We have used a mix of coconut cream and yoghurt in the pannacotta to make it a little less rich. As always with gelatine different brands vary so check the instructions on the

packet and use enough to set 600 ml / 1 pint of liquid. You can switch around the berries at will and frozen will work equally well as fresh (one of those fruit of the forest mixed packs of frozen berries is ideal).

Serves 4-6

3 leaves of gelatine
250 ml / 8 fl oz / 1 cup plain full-fat yoghurt
500 ml / 16 fl oz / 2 cups coconut cream
3 tablespoons boiling water
3 tablespoons of honey
2 tablespoons caster (superfine) sugar
2 tablespoons berry liqueur (optional)
1 star anise
200 g / 7 oz raspberries
200 g / 7 oz blueberries

Soak the gelatine leaves in cold water for 5-10 minutes.

Lightly oil 6 small dariole moulds or one large 600 ml / one pint pudding bowl.

Whisk together the coconut cream and yoghurt. Remove the gelatine leaves from the cold water, squeeze out and add to the boiling water to dissolve. Stir in the honey. Whisk the gelatine and honey mix into the coconut yoghurt and pour into moulds. Refrigerate until set. This will take at least four hours and overnight is fine.

To make the compote put the berry liqueur if using (or 2 tablespoons water if not) in a saucepan large enough to take the fruit. Stir in the sugar and star anise and cook until the sugar just melts. Add the berries, stir to coat and cook gently for 2-3 minutes until the fruit begins to soften and release its juice. Remove from the heat and cool. Remember to take out the star anise before serving.

To serve, unmould the pannacotta and serve in a pool of berry compote.

A Tattered Tart

This is a delightfully easy tart to make as the whole point is that it should have ragged edges. It is basically an American single crust pie, where the edges of the base fold up over the filling to form a semi-covered tart. It is the perfect receptacle for the contents of your foraging basket: bilberries, brambles and mulberries are ideal and can be padded out with apples. You can either stew cooking apples such as Bramleys or use dessert apples if you want a chunkier filling. Gooseberries work well too.

Serves 6

Pastry
500 g / 1 lb / 4 cups plain (all-purpose) flour
1 good pinch of salt
250 g / 8 oz / 2 sticks of very cold butter, cubed
2 egg yolks

Filling

2 tablespoons semolina

750 g / 1 ½ lbs fruit (you will need to stew cooking apples first to soften them but anything else can go straight into the tart)

Caster (superfine) sugar, to taste, probably 2-3 tablespoons, depending on the fruit

Topping

1-2 tablespoons demerara (raw) or granulated sugar

1 tablespoon of milk

Preheat the oven to 200 C / 400 F / Gas 6. Put the flour and salt into a food processor and pulse a couple of times. Add the cubed butter and process until the mixture resembles fine breadcrumbs. If you don't have a food processor just rub the butter into the flour and salt using your fingertips. Add the egg yolks and pulse or mix till just combined. If it is too dry just add a tablespoon of cold water. Turn out onto a floured surface and knead briefly to make a flat round. Wrap in clingfilm (saran wrap) and place in the fridge to rest for half an hour.

Roll out the pastry into a rough oval, about 40 cm / 15 in long. The exact shape doesn't really matter; it just needs to be large enough to accommodate all the fruit with 5-7 cm / 2-3 in spare all round.

Place the pastry on a lightly greased baking tray (cookie sheet). Sprinkle the semolina over the area where the fruit will go (to prevent a soggy bottom). Pile the fruit into the centre and sprinkle with sugar. Bring the edges of the pastry up and over the fruit, squashing the edges together and leaving the centre open. It is meant to look ragged and uneven. Paint the surface of the pastry with milk and sprinkle the sugar onto it.

Place in the oven and cook for about 35 minutes till the crust is golden-brown. The tart can be served hot or cold but either way it need lots of cream.

BAKING

CRANBERRY SCONES

Scones are an essential part of afternoon tea and these are a delicious variation of traditional fruit scones. Make sure the dried cranberries don't have any extra sugar added or your scones will be too sweet. The trick to making really good scones is to be gentle; mix lightly with your fingertips and let the weight of the rolling pin do the flattening; don't push down on the dough.

Makes about 15 scones

450 g / 15 oz / 3 3/5 cups self raising flour
pinch salt
1 tablespoon baking powder
1 tablespoon caster (superfine) sugar
100 g / 3 ½ oz dried cranberries
100 g / 3 ½ oz / 7 tablespoons chilled butter, cut into cubes
300-320 ml / 10 – 11 fl oz / 1 ⅓ cups milk

Preheat the oven to 220 C / 425 F / Gas 7. Lightly grease a baking sheet.

Sift the flour, salt and baking powder into a large bowl and add the sugar and butter. Mix lightly, using your fingertips till the mixture resembles breadcrumbs. This is better done by hand rather than in a mixer as the latter can make the scones stodgy. Add the berries and mix well.

Make a well in the centre and pour in most of the milk. Using a fork, combine the mixture to form a soft, sticky dough. You may not need all the milk. Mix gently and don't handle the dough more than you need or the scones will lose their light texture.

Turn the dough onto a floured surface and form into a disc. Gently roll out till it is about 2.5 cm / 1 in thick. Using a round 6 cm or 8 cm (2 ½ or 3 in) pastry cutter dipped in flour cut the dough, turning the cutter as you push down. This will give the scones rough sides which will allow them to rise better. Place them on the prepared baking sheet and brush the tops with milk to glaze.

Bake the scones for about 15 minutes. Check them after 12 minutes; they should be well risen and just turning golden brown. Cool on a wire rack.

The scones can be served warm or cool, either with cream and jam or the Berry Butter on page 199.

Raspberry Brownies

Brownies are perennially popular and the only thing that could possibly make a brownie better is a berry, of course. We always make these with raspberries but there is no reason why you couldn't use blackberries, mulberries or cranberries instead; we think you need a slightly tart berry to cut through the chocolate.

The key to a good brownie is the cooking time – don't overbake or they become dry and cakey, you want to preserve that unctuous gooeyness in the centre. Cook until just set or when a knife or skewer inserted in the middle comes out with just a few moist crumbs.

You can use frozen raspberries and do not need to defrost them first.

Makes 16

155 g / 50 z / 1 ¼ c plain (all-purpose) flour
¼ tsp salt
110 g / 4 oz good quality plain (bittersweet) chocolate
110 g / 4 oz / 1 stick unsalted butter
150 g / 5 oz / ⅔ cup dark soft brown sugar
150 g / 5oz / ⅔ cup caster (superfine) sugar
2 eggs
125 g / 4 oz fresh or frozen raspberries

Preheat the oven to 180 C / 350 F / Gas 4. Line a 23 cm / 9 in square baking tin (cake pan) with baking parchment.

Sift the flour and salt into a large bowl.

Melt the chocolate and butter in a bain-marie or heatproof bowl set over just boiled water. Add the sugars and leave 5 minutes to dissolve slightly, then stir to mix well.

Beat in the eggs one by one to make a glossy mixture. Add the raspberries and stir through. Gently fold in the flour. You want an even brown coloured mix (not streaky) but don't overmix.

Pour the mixture into the prepared baking tin (cake pan) to form an even layer. Bake for 25-30 minutes or until just set in the middle. A knife inserted in the centre should come out with just a few moist crumbs. Cool completely in the pan before cutting into squares.

Strawberry Meringue Cake

This is, as they say on the Great British Bake Off, a showstopper. It looks really impressive and people always ask how you get the sponge and meringue layers. This is another cake we first met when we were working at Books for Cooks, where the incomparable Marilou used to bake it regularly. The original recipe came from Nigella Lawson's *Forever Summer*. Now we have left Books for Cooks, we have to cook it ourselves but this is no hardship, and it is a much-loved favourite bake.

Serves 8

For the cake
175 g / 6 oz / 1 ¼ cups plain (all-purpose) flour
35 g / 1 ½ oz / 4 tablespoons cornflour (cornstarch)
1 ½ teaspoons baking powder
150 g / 5 oz / 1 ¼ sticks unsalted butter, softened
100 g / 3 ½ oz / ½ cup caster (superfine) sugar
1 teaspoon vanilla essence
5 egg yolks
3 tablespoons milk

For the meringue
5 egg whites
a pinch of salt
200 g / 7 oz / 1 cup caster (superfine) sugar
50 g / 1 ¾ oz / ½ cup flaked almonds

For the filling
375 ml / 13 fl oz / 1 ⅔ cup double (heavy) cream
250 g / 8 oz strawberries, hulled and thickly sliced

Heat the oven to 160 C / 325 F / Gas 3. Butter and line two 24 cm / 9 ½ in springform cake tins.

Sift the flour, cornflour (cornstarch) and baking powder. In another bowl, beat the butter, sugar and vanilla till light and fluffy. Beat in the egg yolks one at a time sprinkling a tablespoon of flour after each egg to stop the mixture curdling. Gently fold in the remaining flour in two batches alternating with the milk to make a light smooth batter. Divide evenly between the two tins. Don't worry if it looks as though there is not much cake mix in each tin - there should be enough to cover the base of the tins, but not much more.

In a new clean grease-free bowl, whisk the egg whites with a pinch of salt until they hold soft slightly drooping peaks. Add the sugar a tablespoon at a time and continue whisking until you have a firm glossy mix. Divide it between the cake tins on top of the cake mix. Sprinkle over the flaked almonds.

Place the cakes in the oven - use the lower half of your oven as the meringue rises up. Bake for 40 minutes or until the meringue is crisp and lightly golden and the sides of the cake have pulled away from the tin. Run a knife around the edge of the cakes to loosen and then cool in the tin on a wire rack.

When you are ready to serve whip the cream until it holds its shape. Put the bottom layer, meringue side down, onto your serving plate and spread evenly with cream, then arrange the sliced strawberries on top. Sit the top layer of the cake on the strawberries, meringue side up. Serve.

Raspberry Red Velvet Cupcakes

These were inspired by a Jo Wheatley recipe for a larger cake. We liked the fact that the colour comes mainly from the raspberries although a little touch of colouring paste makes it redder. Make sure you use paste, not the cheap liquid colours as you need a terrific amount of these to get the colour and this can affect the taste. We have also changed the icing as we love this dark chocolate truffly topping which goes so well with raspberries.

Makes 12

For the cakes
200 g / 7 oz / 1 cup caster sugar
100 g / 3 ½ oz / 7 tablespoons butter
2 eggs
200 g / 7 oz / 1 ½ cups self-raising flour
50 g / 1 ¾ oz / ½ cup cocoa powder
150 ml / 5 fl oz / ⅔ cup unflavoured yoghurt
50 g / 1 ¾ oz full-fat cream cheese
75 g / 2 ½ oz raspberries, puréed and sieved (strained) to

remove seeds
¼ teaspoon red food gel

To decorate
100 g / 3 ½ oz dark (bittersweet) chocolate
75 ml / 2 ¾ fl oz / ⅓ cup double (heavy) cream
75 g / 2 ½ oz / ⅔ sticks unsalted butter
250 g / 8 oz / 1 cup icing sugar
12 raspberries

Heat the oven to 180 C / 350 F / Gas 4. Line a twelve pan cupcake tray with paper cases.

Cream the butter, cream cheese and sugar together until light and fluffy. Sift the flour together with the cocoa powder. Add the eggs one at a time beating well after each addition and adding a tablespoon of the flour mix to prevent curdling.

Add half the remaining flour mix. Mix together the yoghurt, raspberry purée and food colouring. Fold half into the cake batter. Fold in the remaining flour and finally, the remaining yoghurt mix.

Spoon into the cake cases and bake for 20-25 minutes or until a skewer comes out clean. Leave to cool in the tin for 10 minutes, and then turn out onto a rack.

Once the cakes are completely cold, make the icing. Melt the chocolate and cream together over a pan of boiling water. Add in the butter and allow it to melt. Stir well to combine. Add half the icing sugar and stir well to combine. Beat in the remainder of the icing sugar. Pipe or swirl onto the cupcakes and decorate with fresh raspberries.

Strawberry Butterfly Cakes

Before cupcakes there were butterfly cakes and these sweet little strawberry flutterbys will win you back to the originals. They were a must-have at childhood birthday teas and are so deserving of a comeback. You can use your strawberry butter (see page 205) to make the butter cream or just whisk in a few strawberries.

Makes 12

For the cakes
150 g / 5 oz / 1 ¼ cups plain (all purpose) flour
1 teaspoon baking powder
150 g / 5 oz / 1 ¼ sticks of butter
150 g / 5 oz / ¾ cups caster (superfine) sugar
2 eggs
1 teaspoon vanilla essence (extract)
1-2 tablespoons milk

For the icing
140 g / 5 oz / 1 ⅓ stick unsalted butter
280 g / 10 oz / 2 ¼ cups icing (confectioners') sugar
1 – 2 tablespoons of milk
18 – 20 strawberries, hulled and quartered

Preheat your oven to 180 C / 350 F / Gas Mark 4. Line 12 cupcake moulds with paper cases.

Sift together the flour and baking powder. In a separate bowl cream the butter and sugar until light and fluffy. Add the eggs one at a time adding a tablespoon of flour after each egg to prevent the mixture curdling. Stir in the vanilla extract.

Add a third of the flour mixture and beat to combine, add half the milk and beat again. Repeat this process until you have used up the flour and milk. Do not beat too hard or long, just enough to combine, as over beating will make the cakes tough.

Spoon into the cupcake cases and bake for 25 minutes until golden and risen and a fine skewer inserted in the middle of the cake comes out clean. Cool on a rack.

Beat the butter in a large bowl until soft. Add half the icing sugar and 1 tablespoon of milk and beat until smooth. Add the remaining icing sugar and beat until creamy and smooth. Add in the last tablespoon of milk if necessary to loosen the mixture.

Once cool cut a one third off of the top of each cake and then cut this circle into half to give two semi-circular "wings". Put and dollop of buttercream and a couple of sliced strawberries on top of each cake and push the two half circles into the icing at a slight angle to look like wings.

Honeyberry Bakewells

Our version of the traditional Bakewell tart uses honeyberry (haskap) instead of the more traditional raspberry jam. You can use any berry jam you have to hand but we find the sweet/tart mix of the honeyberry goes particularly well with the almond frangipane. Ideally you would use your own chunky home-made honeyberry jam in the tarts but if time is short do use a good quality bought jam. If it is very smooth, pop in a few whole honeyberries (haskaps) to give a good texture (fresh, frozen or dried all work).

We use a deep tartlet tin to make these so you get a good proportion of berry jam to pastry and topping. Ours are 7.5 cm / 3 in across and 3 cm / 1 in deep.

Makes 12

For the pastry
200 g / 7 oz / 1 ¾ cups plain (all purpose) flour
50 g / 2 oz / ½ cups ground almonds
50 g / 2 oz / ½ cups icing (confectioners') sugar
pinch salt
150 g / 5 oz / 10 tablespoons cold unsalted butter, diced
2 egg yolks

For the frangipane
50 g / 1 ¾ oz / 2 tablespoons butter
75 g / 3 oz / ¾ cup ground almonds
75 g / 3 oz / ⅔ cup icing (confectioners') sugar
1 egg
1 tablespoon brandy (optional)
24 teaspoons of good quality berry jam
12 teaspoons flaked almonds

You can make the pastry either in a food processor or by hand. If you are making it by hand, combine the dry ingredients, rub in the butter lightly until the mixture forms dry crumbs then cut in the egg yolks with a knife, working quickly to combine. If the mixture is too dry you can add a drizzle of iced cold water but it probably won't need it. If you are using a food processor, pulse the dry ingredients briefly to combine, add in the cold diced butter, and pulse again until the mixture forms dryish crumbs. Add the egg yolks and give a final quick pulse until the mixture comes together, turn out.

Wrap the pastry in cling film (saran wrap) and put into the fridge for at least 30 minutes to rest. Roll out and cut out twelve circles to line the tartlet tins so the pastry comes about two thirds of the way up the tin. At this point we like to pop the tin in the freezer for half an hour. This way you can bake them directly without having to line the tarts with baking paper and baking beans for the first blind bake.

Preheat your oven to 180 C / 350 F / Gas 4.

Blind bake your tarts for 10 minutes. Remove from the oven. Fill each tart case with two teaspoons of honeyberry (haskap) jam.

Beat the butter, ground almonds, icing (confectioners') sugar, egg and brandy together to form a smooth cream and spoon onto the top of the jam. Sprinkle with flaked almonds and bake for 15 minutes until risen and golden. Cool on a rack.

Blueberry Muffins

A good muffin recipe is like a diamond or a Swiss bank account, it will stand you in good stead for life, although if you have enough diamonds and Swiss banks accounts, you can get someone else to make the muffins.

There are a couple of tricks to muffins, and once you have mastered these, you can mix and match the flavours to suit your mood. The key thing is never to over mix. We find the best way is to have two bowls, one for the dry ingredients and one for the liquids and only to mix the two together at the very last moment, stirring just enough to combine, but never beating.

The recipe below is for blueberry muffins but feel free to vary the flavours at will, just keep your additions to one cup. We have had success with raspberry and white chocolate chip, blackberry with a little lemon zest and honeyberries and a teaspoon of powdered ginger

Makes 9 large muffins or twelve smaller cupcake size

250 g / 8 oz / 2 cups plain (all purpose) flour
½ teaspoon salt
80 g / 2 ½ oz / ⅓ cup caster (superfine) sugar
2 ½ teaspoons baking powder
1 cup blueberries
2 eggs
250 ml / 8 fl oz / 1 cup milk
75 ml / 2 ½ fl oz / ⅓ cup flavourless oil

Blueberry Muffins

Preheat the oven to 225 C / 425 F / Gas 7. Sieve the flour and baking powder together in a large bowl. Add the salt and sugar and the blueberries. Stir to combine.

In a second bowl or measuring jug beat the eggs together with the milk and oil.

Add the liquid mix to the dry ingredients and stir briefly to combine. Spoon into greased or lined muffin tins and bake for 20-25 minutes until golden brown and risen and a skewer or toothpick inserted in the middle of a muffin comes out clean. Leave for a few moments and when cool enough to handle, turn out onto a rack to cool completely.

Gooseberry and Almond Loaf Cake

This makes a great pudding with cream or custard or is fantastic for afternoon tea. The cake is very moist, so put the tin in a baking dish to stop it oozing all over your oven.

125 g / 4 oz / 1 stick butter
175 g / 6 oz / 1 ¼ cups self-raising flour
Pinch of salt
125 g / 4 oz / ⅔ cup caster (superfine) sugar
75 g / 2 ¾ oz / ¾ cup ground almonds
300 g / 10 oz / 2 cups gooseberries, topped and tailed
1 teaspoon almond essence
2 large eggs, beaten
demerara (raw)sugar for dusting

Grease a rectangular cake tin (23 x 9 cm / 9 x 4 in) and line the base with baking parchment. A tin with collapsible sides makes it easier to get the cake out. Preheat the oven to 180 C / 350 F / Gas 4.

Put the flour, salt and butter into a food processor and pulse until it looks like fine breadcrumbs. Transfer the flour mixture to a large bowl and add the sugar and ground almonds. Mix well. Put aside half a dozen or so gooseberries for decoration and add the rest to the bowl. Stir so they are well coated. Add the almond essence and eggs and mix everything together.

Put the mixture into the tin and push the remaining gooseberries into the surface. Bake for 45-50 minutes. The top should be crisp but not too brown. A skewer should come out clean, but remember it may be wet because of the juice from the gooseberries. As soon as the cake comes out of the oven sprinkle the top with demerara (raw) sugar. Leave to cool in the tin on a wire rack before turning out.

MILK CHOCOLATE BRAMBLE CAKE

This is a gentle chocolate cake, rich, but mild in flavour. You need to use dark chocolate in the cake mixture as the flavour of milk chocolate is lost in cooking. For a more intense chocolaty taste, use dark chocolate for the icing too. It is best made with small, foraged blackberries as the large cultivated ones tend to make the cake soggy in parts. Earlier in the summer, raspberries are a delicious alternative.

Milk Chocolate
Bramble Cake

Cake
200 g / 7 oz / 1 ¾ sticks butter
100 g / 3 ½ oz dark (bittersweet) chocolate
4 eggs
200 g / 7 oz / 1 cup caster (superfine) sugar
200 g / 7 oz / 1 ⅔ cups self-raising flour, sifted
175 g / 6 oz / 1 ¼ cups brambles or blackberries

Icing
100 g / 3 ½ oz good quality milk chocolate
140 g / 5 oz / 1 ¼ sticks butter, softened
140 g / 5 oz / 1 cup icing (confectioners') sugar

Preheat the oven to 180 C / 350F / Gas 4. Grease 2 x 20 cm / 8 in loose-bottomed cake tins and line the bases with baking parchment.

To make the cake: Bring a large pan of water to boil. Break the dark (bittersweet) chocolate and put it and the butter into a bain-marie or heatproof bowl which will fit over the pan. Remove the pan of boiling water from the heat, place the bowl of chocolate over it and leave to melt, stirring occasionally. Once the butter and chocolate have melted set aside to cool.

Add eggs and sugar to the chocolate mixture and beat with an electric mixer until smooth. This shouldn't take more than a couple of minutes.

Reserve a handful of the blackberries for decoration and add the rest to the flour. Stir to coat the berries and then gently fold into the chocolate mixture.

Divide the mixture evenly between the two tins and bake for 30-35 minutes. The top should be nicely risen and a skewer should come out pretty well clean. Remember the berries will make the cake juicy.

Remove from the oven, allow the cakes to cool in the tins until you can handle them, 10 minutes or so, and then turn onto a wire rack to cool completely.

To make the icing: Melt the chocolate in a bowl over hot water as before, remove from the heat and set aside to cool.

Beat the butter and icing sugar until creamy and then mix in the melted chocolate.

Level the top of one cake, if necessary, and spread half the icing onto it. Put the other cake on top and spread the remaining icing evenly over the top. Decorate with the reserved berries.

Jassy's Sloe Gin and Walnut Fruit Cake

This is from our extensive collection (we are recipe magpies) of magazine clippings. It is from a back issue of *Delicious Magazine* but unfortunately we can't remember who the lovely Jassy was. Whoever you are, thank you for this truly delicious cake which as well as tasting fabulous, helps to use up the sloe gin lake.

Our only change, in the true berry spirit, has been to substitute dried cranberries for the dried cherries in the original. It makes a great Christmas cake; just cover with marzipan and icing and decorate with frosted cranberries (see page 112).

Serves 10

650 g / 1 lb 5 oz mixed dried fruit (sultanas, currants and raisins)
100 g / 3 ½ oz dried cranberries
zest and juice of one orange
150 ml / 5 fl oz / ⅔ cup sloe gin (plus extra for feeding)
225 g / 8 oz / 2 sticks of unsalted butter
250 g / 8 oz / 1 cup soft light brown sugar
1 tablespoon dark treacle (molasses)
4 medium eggs
250 g / 8 oz / 2 cups plain (all purpose) flour
2 teaspoons ground cinnamon
2 teaspoons mixed spice
100 g / 3 ½ oz / ¾ cup walnuts, roughly chopped

Put all the dried fruit in a large bowl, stir in the orange juice and zest and 150 ml / 5 fl oz / ⅔ cup sloe gin. Cover and leave to soak overnight.

Preheat the oven to 180 C / 325 F / Gas 4. Grease and line a 20 cm / 8 in round cake tin making sure the baking paper around the sides comes 5 cm / 2 in above the tin. Wrap another tall piece of baking paper around the outside of the tin and secure with string. Set the tin onto a baking sheet.

Beat the butter and sugar until fluffy and a pale toffee colour, then beat in the treacle (molasses). Add the beaten eggs one at a time adding a tablespoon of flour after each egg to stop the mixture curdling.

Sift the flour and spices together then stir into the egg mix to give a smooth batter. Add the walnuts, the soaked fruit and any sloe gin left in the bottom of the bowl. Stir to combine.

Pour into the cake tin and bake for 75-90 minutes until firm to the touch and a skewer inserted in the middle comes out clean. Check it a couple of times during the baking and if it is getting too dark on top, cover the cake with baking parchment.

Remove from the oven. Use a skewer to poke a few small holes in the top of the cake and pour over 1 tablespoon of sloe gin. Once cool remove from the tin, wrap in baking paper and then foil. Store in an airtight container. Feed once a week with 1 tablespoon of sloe gin. It will be ready to eat after a week, but is even better after a month and will keep for at least a year.

CRANBERRY AND WHITE CHOCOLATE BISCUITS

For years we've been making Delia Smith's Chocolate Orange Biscuits, which originally appeared in her *Book of Cakes* in 1977. We then started to experiment with berry variations and we think this combination beats even the original, but then we're biased in favour of berries.

Makes two dozen biscuits

125 g / 5 oz / 1 stick butter
175 g / 6 oz / 1 cup caster (superfine) sugar
225 g / 8 oz / 1 ¾ cups plain (all purpose) flour
2 teaspoons baking powder
75 g / 3 oz / ½ cup white chocolate, finely chopped
30 g / 1 oz / ¼ cup dried cranberries
1 tablespoon orange juice

Heat the oven to 180 C / 350 F / Gas 4

Beat the butter and sugar together till pale and creamy. Sift the flour and baking powder and mix well. Add the rest of the ingredients and mix together. You should have a stiff, slightly crumbly dough. Don't be tempted to add too much orange juice.

Lightly flour a work top and roll out the dough to ½ - 1 cm / ¼ - ½ in. It will be very crumbly but that doesn't matter, just squish it together. The biscuits will hold together once cooked. Cut into 5 cm / 2 in rounds and place on a greased baking tray (cookie sheet). Allow an inch or so between the biscuits as they spread a lot. Bake on the top shelf for about 10-15 minutes; the biscuits should be just turning golden brown. Leave to cool on the baking tray (cookie sheet) for a couple of minutes to firm up and then transfer to a wire rack to cool fully. In the unlikely event that any are left, these biscuits can be stored in an airtight tin.

Gooseberry and Elderflower Cake

This is similar to the Gooseberry and Almond Cake on page 162 but even more gooey and sumptuous, with thick elderflower icing cascading down the sides. It is just as good as a pudding as an afternoon tea cake. The cake is very moist so put the tin on a baking tray to stop it oozing all over your oven.

Cake
125 g / 4 oz / 1 stick butter
125 g / 4 oz / ⅔ cup caster (superfine) sugar
2 large eggs, beaten
1 tablespoon elderflower cordial
175 g / 6 oz / 1 ¼ cups self-raising flour
300 g / 10 oz / 2 cups gooseberries, topped and tailed

Icing
115 g / 3 ½ oz / ⅔ cup icing sugar
1-2 tablespoon elderflower cordial

Grease a rectangular cake tin (23 x 9 cm / 9 x 4 in) and line the base with baking parchment. A tin with collapsible sides makes it easier to get the cake out. Heat the oven to 180 C / 350 F / Gas 4.

Cream the butter and sugar together and then add the eggs, one at a time. Beat well after adding each egg so the mixture is smooth and creamy. Beat in the elderflower cordial, sift the flour and gently fold into the mixture. Finally fold in the gooseberries.

Put the mixture into a tin and bake for about 50 minutes. The top should be crisp but not too brown and spring back when pressed down with a finger. The skewer test doesn't work well with this cake because it is so moist. Remove the cake from the oven and as soon as it is cool enough to handle, turn onto a wire rack.

When the cake is cool, sift the icing sugar into a bowl. Add the elderflower cordial a little at a time and mix well with a knife. Add more sugar or cordial to get the thickness you want, ideally the icing should dribble down the sides of the cake, but not run away completely. Spread over the cake with a flat knife or metal spatula.

CHEAT'S MILLE FEUILLE

We love home-made pastry mille feuille, the contrast of crisp pastry, sweet cream and tart berries is unbeatable, but some days (to be honest most days) the idea of making puff pastry and crème pâtissière from scratch is just too daunting. This cheat is still home-made so you don't lose your domestic goddess badge but is much quicker and easier.

Serves 6

6 leaves ready-made filo pastry
50 g / 2 oz / ½ stick butter, melted
50 g / 2 oz / ½ cup golden caster (superfine) sugar
5 tablespoons finely chopped pistachios
400 g / 14 oz raspberries
400 g / 14 oz strawberries, half the quantity chopped
250 g / 8 oz / 1 cup mascarpone
250 ml / 8 oz / 1 cup crème fraiche
300 ml / ½ pint / 1 ½ cups double cream

Heat the oven to 200 C /400 F / Gas 6. Line two baking trays (cookie sheets) with non-stick baking paper. Mix the golden caster (superfine) sugar and the finely chopped pistachios together in a small bowl.

Lay one sheet of filo on each of the two lined trays (sheets). Brush with melted butter and sprinkle each with some of the sugar pistachios. Lay another sheet of filo on top of the first and repeat, lay on the final sheet of filo brush with butter and sprinkle with the last of the sugar pistachios. Press down gently and bake in the oven for about seven minutes or until golden and crisp.

Cut each sheet into 9 even sized rectangles and set on a rack to cool whilst you make the filling.

Put half the raspberries and all of the chopped strawberries in a bowl and crush with a fork. Beat the mascarpone, crème fraiche and double cream together until smooth and fold in the crushed fruit. You can then either pipe or dollop the fruit cream onto 6 filo rectangles, place another filo rectangle on top then another layer of fruit cream finishing with a filo rectangle.

Serve with a few of the remaining whole fruits tumbled prettily beside the mille feuille. A drizzle of fruit coulis is also nice if you have some ready to hand.

You can make the cream and pastry ahead of time but assemble shortly before you eat or they will go soft.

Berries for Supper

A Simple Side Salad

Sometimes you just need a simple little side salad. Something that tastes delicious but won't upstage your star dish and this is just the ticket. The cranberries and walnuts lift it out of the ordinary and the mustardy dressing and mix of leaves means it cuts through the richness of a quiche. Perfect then with Jane's favourite French Onion Tart.

You can vary the leaves depending on what you have to hand but we think a little rocket (arugula) or frisée lettuce (chicory) mixed in with cos or buttercrunch makes the ideal combination of sweet and bitter.

We have given amounts here as a guide, but as with all salads, a handful of this and a handful of that is really the way to go.

You can prepare the salad and the dressing ahead of time but keep them separate and combine just before serving.

Serves 4-6 as a side salad

1 head of cos or buttercrunch lettuce
100 g / 4 oz rocket (arugula) leaves
30 g / 1 oz / ¼ cup coarsely chopped walnuts
30 g / 1 oz / ¼ cup dried cranberries
sea salt and black pepper
45 ml / 1 ½ fl oz / 3 tablespoons olive oil
15 ml / ½ fl oz / 1 tablespoon balsamic vinegar
15 ml / ½ fl oz / 1 tablespoon grain mustard
pinch of caster (superfine) sugar

Wash the leaves and dry well in a salad spinner or clean tea towel. Tear into bite-size pieces and place in the serving bowl. Add the walnuts and cranberries and season to taste with freshly ground sea salt and black pepper.

Whisk the dressing ingredients together until they emulsify. When ready to serve drizzle over the salad and toss to combine.

BARLEY AND ARTICHOKE SALAD WITH RASPBERRY DRESSING

This is a robust salad which travels well so is ideal for picnics or lunch "al desko". The combination of grains and goji berries makes it both filling and good for you.

The raspberry dressing is delicious and a tremendously vibrant girly pink colour. The quantities given make a little more than you need for this recipe, but it will keep a few days in the fridge and you can use it on other salads (it is great on a simple spinach and pecan salad). If you don't have raspberry vinegar, you can use cider vinegar but the raspberry vinegar really enhances the berry flavour and is worth seeking out or making your own (see page 201).

Serves 4 as side salad or for a picnic or 2 for a main meal

150 g / 5 oz pearl barley
15 g / ½ oz goji berries
100 g / 3 ½ oz char-grilled artichoke hearts, quartered
45 g / 1 ½ oz sun-dried tomatoes, chopped
3 spring (green) onions, white part only
1 teaspoon chilli flakes
2 large handfuls of baby spinach
3 sprigs of fresh mint
60 g / 2 oz feta cheese, crumbled

For the dressing
45 g / 1 ½ oz fresh raspberries
1 teaspoon lemon juice
2 teaspoons raspberry vinegar
1 tablespoon honey
3 teaspoons olive oil

To make the dressing put all of the ingredients into a small blender and whiz to combine.

Put the pearl barley in a saucepan, cover generously with water and bring to the boil. Turn down the heat and simmer for 20-30 minutes or until tender. Once cooked drain, rinse in cold water to stop the barley cooking and transfer to a large bowl. Add half the raspberry dressing and toss to combine. Season to taste with freshly ground sea salt and black pepper.

Soak the goji berries in a little boiling water from a kettle for 5-10 minutes to soften, then drain.

Chop the spring (green) onions and shred the spinach. Roll the mint leaves and cut into fine ribbons. Add all of the salad ingredients except the feta to the cooked pearl barley. Toss to combine. Sprinkle the feta over the top and drizzle with a little more of the dressing.

CHICKEN BARBERRY PILAU

This is a great dish to make the day after you have roasted a chicken, but if you don't have any ready-cooked chicken to hand, just poach a chicken breast and use that. The tartness of the barberries really lifts this dish and they can be bought online or from a Middle Eastern food store but, if you find them difficult to get, cranberries also work well and don't need soaking.

Serves 2

2 tablespoons unsalted butter
1 shallot, finely chopped
1 medium courgette (zucchini), diced
150 g / 5 oz brown basmati rice
750 ml / 1 ¼ pint / 3 cups chicken stock, preferably home-made
pinch of saffron
salt and pepper
30 g / 1 oz barberries or cranberries
150 g / 5 oz cooked chicken, cut into bite-size pieces
2 tablespoons chopped dill fronds
2 tablespoons chopped almonds

Cover the barberries with boiling water and leave to soak whilst you prepare the rice.

Melt the butter in a deep frying pan (skillet) which has a lid. Add the shallot and courgette (zucchini) and fry for 5 minutes or till softened, but not coloured. Add the rice and stir so the buttery juices coat the rice. Add the chicken stock and the saffron. Mix well and cover with the lid and leave to cook on a very low heat for 20-30 minutes, or until the stock is absorbed. Taste the rice, it should be tender. If not you may need to add a little more stock (or water) and cook for another 10 minutes or so until completely tender but not mushy. Season to taste with freshly ground sea salt and black pepper.

Stir in the chicken. Drain the barberries and add to the pilau.

Continue to cook until heated through. Garnish with dill fronds and almonds and serve.

Cranberry Roast Ham with Cranberry Beetroot Relish

The ham is delicious hot or cold and makes a great Thanksgiving or Christmas Eve supper for friends. If you are cooking this for Christmas Eve, you can hold back (hide if necessary) enough slices to accompany the Christmas dinner. Wrap them in tin foil and warm through in the oven whilst you are making the turkey gravy on the big day. Keep any leftover relish to go into the turkey and ham sandwiches on Christmas night. Sally's brother thinks that turkey and ham sandwiches are the best part of Christmas Day and always insists on them, even when he can't possibly want to eat anything more.

A ham is a gammon until it is cooked when it becomes a ham.

Cranberry Glazed Ham

Feeds 6 with leftovers

For the ham
2 kg / 2 ½ lb unsmoked boneless gammon, skin-on

2 litres / 2 ½ pints / 8 cups cranberry juice
2 sticks celery
1 carrot
1 onion, peeled and halved
a few black peppercorns
10 juniper berries
2 bay leaves

For the glaze
100 g / 3 ½ oz / ½ cup demerara (raw) sugar
60 ml / 2 fl oz / ¼ cup Madeira
30 ml / 1 fl oz / 2 tablespoons sherry vinegar
125 g / 4 oz honey
Whole cloves to decorate

For the relish
300 ml / 10 fl oz / 1 ¼ cups water
450 g / 1lb / 4 ½ cups cranberries (fresh or frozen, dried at a pinch)
100 g / 3 ½ oz / ½ cup caster (superfine) sugar
1 apple, grated
2 whole chillies, deseeded and finely chopped
4 tablespoons cider vinegar
250 g / 8 oz cooked beetroot (beets), cut into small dice
3 tablespoons cranberry jelly (preferably home-made)

Place the gammon in a large saucepan, cover with water, bring to the boil and then throw the water away. Rinse the gammon and the pot and put the gammon back in the pot. Add the vegetables, peppercorns, juniper berries and bay leaves and pour in the cranberry juice. If it doesn't quite cover the gammon top it up with water.

Bring to the boil and turn down the heat to a gentle simmer. Keep simmering for 1 ½ to 2 hours or until tender. Keep checking from time to time and if necessary top up the water and skim off any froth that rises to the top. Let it cool in the water.

Meanwhile get on with the relish. Place the water, cranberries, sugar, chillies and vinegar into a pan over a medium heat. Gradually bring to the boil, turn down the heat and simmer for 10-15 minutes or until the mixture thickens. Add the beetroot (beets) and the cranberry jelly and cook for another 5 minutes stirring. Leave to cool. Serve at room temperature.

Preheat the oven to 190 C / 375 F / Gas 5. Put all the glaze ingredients in a small saucepan and stir over a low heat to dissolve the sugar. Bring to the boil and simmer for 5-10 minutes to make a dark glossy syrup. Put the ham in a roasting tray large enough for it to fit comfortably and carefully cut away the skin leaving as much of the fat as possible. Score the fat in a criss-cross diamond pattern. Stud each diamond with a clove. Discard the poaching liquid.

Pour half the glaze over the ham and roast for 15 minutes. Pour or brush on the remainder of the glaze and roast for another 25-35 minutes or until golden brown basting occasionally with the pan juices.

Let the ham rest for 15 minutes and serve if eating hot, or let cool completely to serve cold.

HALIBUT WITH STRAWBERRY CHIPOTLE GLAZE AND STRAWBERRY SALSA

This sounds a little unusual but trust us it is delicious. The sweetness of the strawberry combined with the smoky heat of the chilli works so well against the fish. If you don't have halibut, any large flake, firm textured white fish will work as well.

The heat varies between different brands of chipotle paste and what you are looking for here is a subtle smokiness with a kick, not an overwhelming chilli burn. You want to be able to taste the strawberry and the fish so we advise starting with ½ teaspoon of paste in your glaze and then taste - you can always add more in but it is difficult to take it out.

Serves 4

For the glaze
1 shallot
6 strawberries
½ - 1 ½ teaspoons chipotle paste
½ teaspoon dark muscovado sugar
4 x 150 g / 5 oz fillets of halibut, skinned
4 tablespoons pumpkin seeds

For the salsa
1 avocado
3 spring (green) onions
juice of a lime
1 red chilli, seeded and chopped
6 strawberries
2 tablespoons coriander (cilantro), chopped

Preheat the oven to 200 C / 400 F / Gas Mark 6.

First make the glaze. Roughly chop the shallot and strawberries and place all the glaze ingredients in a blender and whiz to a fine purée. Taste and add more chilli if you think it needs it (see note above).

Place the halibut fillets on a lightly oiled baking tray (baking sheet) and brush the glaze over to give a thick pink layer. Sprinkle with the pumpkin seeds. Bake for 10 –15 minutes until cooked through. The timing may vary a little, depending on the thickness of your fillet.

Whilst the fish is cooking, prepare the salsa. Peel, stone and dice the avocado and pour over the lime juice. Hull and dice the strawberries and add these to the avocado. Chop the spring (green) onions and add along with the chopped chilli and coriander. Stir everything together gently.

Serve the fish accompanied by the salsa. We like to serve this with a green salad and a few rosemary potatoes.

A duck crown is a perfect size for two people. This one is roasted simply with a maple glaze to allow the flavour of the sauce to really shine.

If you don't have any red wine open, by all means use double the quantity of port but the sauce will be heavier.

Serves 2-3

1 duck crown
3 tablespoons maple syrup
salt and pepper

For the sauce
1 tablespoon unsalted butter (plus a knob of butter to finish the sauce)
1 shallot
1 tablespoon juniper berries, crushed
150 ml / 5 fl oz / ⅔ cup red wine
150 ml / 5 fl oz / ⅔ cup port
150 ml / 5 fl oz / ⅔ cup chicken or duck stock
1 tablespoon rosemary, finely chopped
150 g / 5 oz blackberries (fresh or frozen)

Preheat the oven to 200 C / 400 F / Gas 6. Season the duck and place on a rack in a roasting tray just large enough to hold the duck. Pour over 2 tablespoons of the maple syrup.

Roast the duck crown for 50 minutes. 20 minutes before the end, baste the breast with the remaining tablespoon of maple syrup. Remove from the oven and rest for 15 minutes in a warm place before serving.

Whilst the duck is roasting, get on with the sauce. Finely chop the shallot and fry in 1 tablespoon of butter until soft but not coloured. Add the port, red wine and crushed juniper berries and boil until the liquid has reduced by half. Add the stock and reduce by half again. Add the blackberries, any residual juice and the chopped rosemary and simmer gently until slightly thickened. Stir in a knob of butter, to give a glossy finish.

JUNIPER POTATOES

This is a twist on the classic potato dauphinoise and we find the addition of juniper makes it the perfect accompaniment for roast or casseroled game.

Serves 4

500 g / 1 lb baking potatoes (we like Maris Piper)
15 g / ½ oz / 1 tablespoon butter
250 ml / 8 fl oz / 1 cup milk
125 g / 4 fl oz / ½ cup double (heavy) cream
1 onion
1 tablespoon juniper berries, crushed
salt & pepper

Preheat the oven to 200 C / 400 F / Gas 6.

Peel the potatoes and slice them very thinly. The easiest way is with a mandolin but if you don't have one then use a sharp knife and a steady hand. Peel and half the onion and slice the halves into thin half moons.

Put the potatoes into a saucepan with the milk and cream and bring up to the boil. Simmer for a minute or two. You are just par cooking them, you don't want them to cook through and break up.

Butter a gratin dish and place one third of the potatoes and milk in a layer in the dish. Strew over half the sliced onion and sprinkle with crushed juniper berries and salt and pepper. Repeat twice more to use up the potato mix – there will not be any onions on top.

Put into the oven and bake for 45 minutes until golden and

bubbling. A sharp knife point poked into the gratin will test that the potatoes are cooked through. This will hold well until the main course is ready, cover with foil if necessary so the top doesn't overbrown.

Red Cabbage with Cranberries

We always serve this with the Christmas turkey. It is totally forgiving and will sit around or can indeed be made the day before and reheated, and the colour is pleasantly festive.

The key to cooking red cabbage is to remember it is a kind of vegetable litmus paper. Acid keeps it red and alkali turns it an unappetising grey. This means that you should always make sure your braising liquid is sufficiently acidic to hold the colour. Cook it in red wine or port, balsamic vinegar or at a pinch water which has a hefty dose of lemon juice added, and your red cabbage will remain gloriously red.

As a bonus, if you have any leftovers from this recipe, and you may, it makes a lot, then mix in a little chopped salami and use some shop-bought puff pastry to make little pasties. Glaze and bake in a hot oven for 30 minutes and serve hot or cold. They used to serve these at a little Lunch Bar on the Plimmer Steps in Wellington, New Zealand and Sally was totally addicted; now she lives in London, she has to make her own.

Serves 6-8

3 tablespoons unsalted butter
2 onions
a pinch of salt
1 medium red cabbage
200 ml / 7 fl oz / 1 cup port or red wine
3 tablespoons balsamic vinegar
100 g / 3 ½ oz / ½ cup brown sugar
200 g / 7 oz cranberries, fresh or frozen
1 teaspoon fennel seeds

Peel and halve the onions and slice them into fine half moons. Shred the cabbage, either cut in half and finely slice or put chunks through the shredding attachment on the food processor.

Melt the butter in a pan large enough to take the cabbage and cook the onions over a low heat with a pinch of salt until softened. Add the cabbage and stir to cover with the buttery juices. Add in the port, vinegar and sugar and turn the heat down as low as you can. Simmer very gently for an hour and a half (a little longer won't matter) but do keep an eye on it, you don't want it to boil dry. Top up with more liquid if required.

Ten minutes before you want to serve, throw in the cranberries and fennel seeds, give an enthusiastic stir and let it heat through.

Huckleberry's Ribs

This is a bit of poetic licence on our part, as of course these delicious finger-licking ribs don't actually use huckleberries at all but rather the delightful honeyberries (haskaps). Indeed, for speed and convenience, we use ready-made honeyberry (haskap) juice although of course you can juice the berries yourself. However, the recipe has a charming Mississippi feel to it, possibly due to the addition of a shot of Bourbon and so we named it Huckleberry's Ribs after Huckleberry Finn, a favourite childhood book. If you can't get honeyberries you can use cranberries.

Serves 6

2 kg / 4 lb of pork spare ribs
1 onion, diced
2 carrots diced
3 ribs of celery, diced
6 cloves of garlic, roughly chopped
3 tablespoons Dijon mustard
4 tablespoons brown sugar
2 tablespoons smoked paprika

2 tablespoons tomato paste
2 cups honeyberry (haskap) juice
dash of tabasco
3 tablespoons Bourbon (optional)

Preheat the oven to 150 C / 300 F / Gas 2.

Place the ribs in a roasting or braising dish large enough to hold all the ribs in one layer. Place the remaining ingredients, except the Bourbon, in a saucepan over a medium heat. Stir until the sugar is dissolved, bring to the boil then add the Bourbon and pour over the ribs. Cover the dish tightly with tin (aluminium) foil and place in the oven.

Check after an hour and a half. You want the meat to be soft but not falling off the bone. Once the meat is soft, remove the ribs from the cooking liquid and set aside. Liquidize the cooking liquid to give a smooth purée then pour this into a saucepan, bring to the boil and simmer until reduced and thick, this will be your coating sauce for the ribs. You can carry on with the recipe now or keep the ribs and basting liquid in the fridge for up to 24 hours until you are ready for the final step. Return to room temperature for the final cooking.

You can cook the ribs in the oven or on a barbecue. If you are using an oven, preheat to 220 C / 425 F / Gas 7. Place the ribs in a single layer on a baking tray (sheet) and brush liberally with the glaze. Cook for 15 minutes, turn over and brush again with the remaining glaze and cook for a final 15 minutes until hot through and slightly caramelized on the edges. If you are cooking on the barbecue, cook over white hot coals basting with the glaze until hot through and slightly caramelized on the edges.

Serve with a tangy slaw and cornbread.

Cranberry Glazed Sausages

Little cranberry-glazed sausages make a perfect Christmas canapé or you can serve them around the turkey at Thanksgiving. We haven't given a portion size for these as we have found people's capacity for eating little sausages is infinite, especially if there are drinks being served. Make as many as you like, we guarantee they will get eaten.

Makes 24

24 cocktail sausages
3 tablespoons cranberry sauce or cranberry jelly
1 teaspoon grated ginger
1 tablespoon water

Preheat your oven to 200 C / 400 F / Gas 6. Melt the cranberry sauce in a small pan with the water and stir in the grated ginger. Remove from the heat. Place the sausages on an oiled baking tray, pour over the sauce and stir to fully coat and bake for 15-20 minutes until cooked through. Serve on a platter with cocktail sticks for spearing.

Chicken Liver Pâté with Berry Glaze

This is very easy to make and is a lovely thing to offer guests with some crusty bread and a simple salad (see page 170 for the cranberry and walnut salad which would be perfect). The glaze looks beautiful but also helps to preserve the pâté, which will keep for a week in the fridge. The glaze makes enough to cover the whole terrine if you make a large one, and is a little too much for the four baby pots but it is not really practical to make this in smaller amounts, so I am afraid you will need to resign yourself to a little waste.

Makes 4 x 200 ml / 7 fl oz / ¾ cup ramekins or one 800ml / 1 ¼ pint terrine dish

For the pâté
175 g / 6 oz / 1 ½ sticks of butter
450 g / 1 lb chicken livers, trimmed and cleaned
2 shallots, finely diced

2 cloves of garlic, crushed with a generous pinch of salt
2 tablespoons sloe gin
2 teaspoon anchovy essence (optional)

For the glaze
250 ml / 8 fl oz / 1 cup cranberry or honeyberry (haskap) juice
3 tablespoons sloe gin
1 tablespoon powdered gelatine

If you are making this in a large terrine dish, line the dish with cling film (saran wrap) leaving enough over the edges to fold over the filled terrine. If you are making a serving in small pots, just butter or oil the pots lightly.

Heat 15 g / ½ oz of butter in a frying pan (skillet) over a medium high heat, add half the livers and fry quickly until golden brown on the outside but still pink in the middle (3-5 minutes). Remove from the pan and put into a food processor. Heat another 15 g / ½ oz of butter and repeat with the remaining livers.

Turn down the heat and melt a third quantity of butter and fry the shallots and garlic until soft but not coloured. Deglaze the pan with the sloe gin and anchovy essence, if using. Add everything to the livers already in the processor plus the remaining butter and blend until smooth.

At this point if you like your pâté silky smooth, then you can pass it through a fine metal sieve (strainer). To be honest, we seldom bother as we favour a more rustic texture. Put into the terrine dish or small pots and cover with cling film and place in the refrigerator to set.

Heat up the berry juice to just below boiling point and remove from the heat. Add the sloe gin and sprinkle over the gelatine. Stir to combine. Leave 10-15 minutes until cool. Pour over the top of the pâté. Return to the fridge for at least a couple of hours, overnight is fine, to set completely. To unmould the large terrine use the cling film (saran wrap) to gently lift the terrine from the dish and place onto a flat oblong plate. The small pots can be taken to the table as is.

Pork and Juniper Terrine

Don't be intimidated by the thought of terrine, it is just meatloaf with attitude. This has a lovely junipery flavour which marries perfectly with the pork. It makes a great picnic dish as it is robust enough to travel well and slices like a dream. Pair it with some cornichons and/ or a chunky fruity pickle. You can also fry up leftover slices in a little oil or butter and serve warm for supper with the hedgerow ketchup on page 197.

The junipery spice blend makes more than you need but it is difficult to make less and it will keep for ages in an airtight jar. You can use it up in casseroles, particularly ones using game or in a meatloaf.

Feeds 8-10 as part of a picnic

For the spice blend
2 teaspoons juniper berries
1 teaspoon whole allspice
1 teaspoon black peppercorns
1 teaspoon coriander seeds
1 teaspoon chilli flakes

250 g / 8 oz Parma ham slices
500 g / 1 lb pork mince
250 g / 8 oz chicken livers, cleaned and trimmed
125 g / 4 oz streaky bacon, finely chopped
250 g / 8 oz pork back fat, finely minced
4 cloves of garlic, crushed with a teaspoon of salt
125 g / 4 oz coarse breadcrumbs
60 g / 2 oz pistachio nuts, shelled

To make the spice blend, put all of the spices into a spice grinder or mini processor and whiz to a fine powder. You can also place in mortar and pestle and grind to a fine powder.

Preheat your oven to 150 C / 300 F / Gas 2. Line a 1.5 litre /

3 pint / 6 cup terrine dish or loaf tin with cling film (saran wrap) leaving enough hanging out over the edges to cover the terrine.

Lay slices of Parma ham across the terrine dish edge to edge lining the bottom and sides of the dish.

Put the pork mince, livers, bacon and back fat into a large bowl. Add the garlic and 1 tablespoon of the spice blend, breadcrumbs and pistachios. Mix together thoroughly. The best way to do this is with your (clean, obviously) hands.

Pack into the Parma-ham-lined mould pressing down well. Cover with any remaining Parma ham. Fold over the overhanging cling film (saran wrap). If your dish has a lid put this on now, if not wrap in tin (aluminium) foil. Stand the dish in a larger baking dish and fill this with boiling water from the kettle to come half way up the sides of the terrine dish.

Place in the oven and cook for one hour. Remove from the oven and place the terrine dish on a rack to cool to room temperature. Now weigh it down; we put a layer of foil on top and then stand baked bean tins on it, and chill for a couple of hours or overnight.

When ready to serve, turn out of the tin onto an oblong dish and remove the cling film (saran wrap). Serve in thick slices.

Cucumber, Feta and Blueberry Salad

This is a light summery salad perfect for lunch with some cold ham. If you have a spiralizer then the long threads of cucumber look particularly pretty but if you don't, it will taste just as good with the cucumber seeded and cubed.

Serves 2

1 clove of garlic
pinch sea salt
85 g / 3 oz blueberries
1 tablespoon extra virgin olive oil
2 teaspoons balsamic vinegar

1 cucumber
85 g / 3 oz bag of mixed salad leaves (we like a watercress and
spinach mix)
1 avocado, peeled, diced and tossed with a little lemon juice
85 g / 3 oz feta cheese, crumbled

Crush the garlic with a pinch of sea salt. Mash or whiz half the blueberries with the oil, vinegar and some black pepper and stir in the crushed garlic.

Spiralize the cucumber or slice into fine ribbons using a vegetable or julienne peeler. Discard the seeds in the centre. Place in the serving bowl and toss with the salad leaves, avocado, feta cheese and remaining blueberries. Drizzle over the dressing.

CRUMBED GOAT'S CHEESE AND BLACKBERRY SALAD

This one is for Sally's father who loved cheese of any description and who always ordered crumbed camembert when it was offered. We have updated the concept a little and made a fresh, fruity salad ideal for lunch preferably eaten out in the garden watching your berries grow. We know he would have approved. There are lots of different goat's cheeses available just pick one you like. We favour a firm white cheese.

Serves 4

2 tablespoons of flour
4 slices of goat's cheese, each about 75 g / 2 ½ oz
1 egg
breadcrumbs for coating
2 large handfuls of mixed salad leaves (red oak leaf lettuce,
lambs lettuce and rocket is nice)
1 handful of green beans, blanched and refreshed in iced water
1 handful of green peas (just podded and raw if very young,
otherwise blanched and refreshed in iced water)

175 g / 6 oz blackberries
oil for frying

For the dressing
50 g / 2 oz blackberries
2 tablespoons olive oil
3 tablespoons red wine vinegar (if you have blackberry vinegar
go all out and use that)
2 teaspoons Dijon mustard
1 tablespoon blackberry jam or jelly
2 shallots, finely chopped

Put the flour, seasoned with a little salt and pepper, in a bowl and toss the goat's cheese pieces in it. Beat the egg in another small bowl and place the breadcrumbs in a third. Dip the floured cheese in the egg and then the breadcrumbs to coat evenly. Place in the fridge until needed.

Crush the blackberries with a fork. Whisk together the oil, vinegar, mustard and jam. Stir in the crushed blackberries and the finely chopped shallots. Season to taste. Keep aside to dress the salad at the end.

Toss the remaining salad ingredients together and divide between four plates.

In a pan large enough to hold the goat's cheese slices in one layer, heat up enough oil to fill the pan to a depth of 2.5 cm / 1 in. When the oil is hot add the goat's cheese and cook till golden on one side. Flip and cook the second side. Remove from the pan and drain on kitchen paper.

Sit a slice of crumbed cheese on each salad plate and drizzle with the dressing.

CRANBERRY SAUCE

This is Nigella's cranberry sauce recipe from that must-have cookbook *Nigella's Christmas*. It is the one we use every year to accompany the Christmas turkey as it foolproof and there is enough stress on Christmas Day without making complicated sauces. If you want to get ahead of yourself you can even make it the day before and serve cold or just put all the ingredients in a small pan and have ready and waiting by the stove. It will take no time at all to cook whilst the turkey is resting.

350 g / 12 oz fresh cranberries
200 g / 7 oz / 1 cup caster (superfine) sugar
45 ml / 1 ½ fl oz / 3 tablespoons cherry brandy
75 ml / 2 ½ fl oz / ⅓ cup water

Put everything in a small saucepan, bring up to the boil and let it bubble away, stirring occasionally, until the sugar is dissolved and the berries start to pop. This will take about ten minutes. Remove from the heat and put into your serving bowl. It will thicken up as it cools.

Braised Chicken with Shitake Mushrooms and Goji Berries

This is ultimate feel good food taking a traditional Chinese dish of chicken and goji berries and making it even more comforting and healthy with the addition of low calorie, vitamin-rich sweet potatoes. With all that vitamin C this is ideal to ward off a threatened cold or just to cheer you up on a cold winter evening. You can substitute the fresh shitakes for a half cup of dried shitake mushrooms, soaked in boiling water for half an hour then drained and chopped.

Serves 4

2-3 tablespoons olive oil
6 chicken thighs, skinless and boneless
1 medium onion, finely chopped
1 green chilli, chopped (de seeded if you don't like chilli heat)
1 tablespoon grated ginger

2 medium sweet potatoes, peeled and chopped
1 cup fresh shitake mushrooms, sliced
250 ml / 8 fl oz / 1 cup chicken stock, ideally home-made

Heat the oil in a large heavy bottomed frying pan (skillet). Fry (sauté) the chopped chicken in small batches until golden, you are just giving the chicken some colour, it doesn't need to be cooked through. Remove the chicken and set aside. Add a little more oil to the pan if necessary.

Fry (sauté) the chopped onion, chilli and ginger until the onion softens. Add the garlic and fry (sauté) one more minute. Add the sweet potatoes and mushrooms and cook gently for 2-3 minutes. Return the chicken to the pan, add the stock and goji berries and bring up to simmering point. Simmer gently for 15 to 20 minutes or until the sweet potatoes are tender and the chicken is cooked through.

Serve on steamed brown rice.

PRESERVING THE HARVEST

FREEZING BERRIES

Of course the best way to enjoy your berries is fresh picked from the garden but if you have a glut, either from a successful growing season or an over-enthusiastic session at the local pick-your-own, then most berries (strawberries excepted) freeze really well. You can often use berries directly from the freezer. This works particularly well for smoothies or in baking when you want whole berries but if you are going to defrost them first, do remember that they will loose their shape and some of their juice as they defrost, so it is a good idea to place the bags of frozen berries on a plate or bowl to defrost, in case the bags leak (they always do). Berry juices can stain your work top irretrievably.

Start with sound, unblemished fruit, if berries are bruised or past their best freezing is not going to improve the situation.

Place the fruit in a single layer on a baking tray (cookie sheet), ideally one with raised edges so no errant berries skid off to lurk in the corners of your freezer. Place the baking tray (cookie sheet) into the freezer, keeping it level, and freeze until the fruit is solid.

Remove from the freezer and transfer the berries into plastic freezer bags or other freezer containers. Label the bags with the name of berry and date of freezing and keep for up to a year.

You can also make berry purée and freeze in ice cube trays for later use in sauces, ice creams and as a quick coolie. Strawberries, which freeze badly as whole fruit, work well as a purée. Just whiz the berries in the food processor, if they have a lot of seeds (like raspberries) push them through a sieve (strainer) and discard the seeds. Then pour into ice cube trays and freeze.

Dehydrating Berries

You can dry any berry, but the best results are from strawberries and whole single berries like blueberries, cranberries or honeyberries. Drupes (raspberries, blackberries etc) are basically little bags of juice and although they will dry eventually, life is too short to wait for them to do so.

Dehydrating intensifies the colour and flavour of the berry and the resulting product is ideal for using in muesli and bars or for your own trail mix. Strawberries should be hulled and either halved or thickly sliced (at least ¼ in thick) but other berries should be dehydrated whole.

You can use a commercial dehydrator or your oven on its lowest setting; fan ovens are particularly good for this. Bear in mind dehydration is a long slow process and it will tie up your oven for hours.

As always, start with sound, unblemished fruit. Squashed berries will stick to the dehydrator trays.

Arrange the fruit on the dehydrator trays or on lined baking trays (cookie sheets) in a single layer and not touching. If you are using an oven then set it to 45-55 C / 113-130 F / Gas ¼. If your oven doesn't go this low set it to the lowest setting and leave the door cracked open.

Place in the dehydrator for 10-12 hours or overnight or the oven for 6-8 hours. The fruit should be completely dry. If you are unsure break or cut a fruit in half to check the inside.

When the fruit is completely cool, store in jars or boxes. It is essential that the fruit is completely dry and cool before you put the lid on your chosen container, as if not you will get condensation which will ruin your dried berries.

Fruit Leather

Fruit leather is a fun product and ideal for children's (or grown-ups) lunchboxes. It is essentially rollable, windable strips of pure fruit flavour. We keep little snap-lock boxes of it in the desk drawer for an afternoon hit of pure berry energy.

Strawberry Leather

Makes 18 finger width rolls

300 g / 10 oz Bramley (cooking) apples, peeled, cored and cut into chunks.
500 g / 1 lb strawberries, hulled

If you are using an oven preheat the oven to 50 C / 120 F / Gas ¼. Line a baking tray (baking sheet) with very lightly oiled greaseproof paper. If you are using a dehydrator lightly oil the plastic sheet.

Put the fruit into a pan with a lid and cook, covered over a medium heat until completely soft (about 10 minutes). Press the pulp through a sieve (strainer) to remove any seeds.

Spread this purée onto the prepared baking tray (sheet) (or the plastic sheet if you are using a dehydrator) in an even 5 mm / 1/6 in layer. Put into the oven or dehydrator and leave for 10-12 hours. It should feel dry and leathery to the touch when ready.

Peel off the paper and cut into strips (we have found this is best done with a pair of scissors). Store in an airtight container for 2-3 weeks.

JAM MAKING

Simone de Beauvoir described jam making as akin to poetry 'With her fire going woman becomes a sorceress ....There is enchantment in these alchemies, there is poetry in making preserves; the housewife has caught duration in the snare of sugar, she has enclosed life in jars.' Indeed there is little which beats the satisfaction of standing in front of a larder packed with jewelled coloured jars of your own preserves or having a jar of something homemade to pass on as a gift.

It is a universal truth that berries make amazing jam. The only downside is that many, especially the perennially popular strawberry, are very low in natural pectin, so you may need to add a little (or use jam sugar) to ensure a good set.

Provided you bear in mind one or two points, making jams and jellies is perfectly simple and incredibly satisfying. Similar principles apply to both jams and jellies and the instructions below apply to both although we refer only to jam.

There are really only two ingredients in jam; fruit and sugar, and so it is important to select these carefully. The appearance of the berry is unimportant, as it will be cooked down but bruised or mouldy fruit will simply not do. Slightly less ripe fruit is preferable for jam making as the pectin levels, which affect the set, will be higher. The type of sugar you use will not affect the taste of the jam but it will affect how it sets and this is why we prefer to use cane rather than beet sugar.

Sugar is present in most plants to varying degrees but commercial sugar production is either from sugar cane or sugar beet. Sugar cane is a grass which grows in warm, moist and tropical conditions whilst sugar beet is a root which prefers more temperate zones. Production of sugar from cane has been going on for centuries with the first known reference to "honey without bees" being made by an officer in the army of Alexander the Great in 325 BC. The Crusaders brought sugar, or "sweet salt" as they called it, back from the Holy Land but widespread European consumption really expanded alongside colonization. Sugar from beets is comparatively more recent, dating from 1747 when German Andreas Maggraf discovered both the sucrose content of sugar beet and a method of extracting it using alcohol. In chemical terms there is little or no difference in the sucrose produced although cane sugar has a lower melting point and is less likely to foam up.

If you are considering the greener choice, cane is the more sustainable crop. Cane stalks are cut for processing, leaving the root intact to grow another day, whilst beets are annuals and hence are resown each year and as they are prone to pests and disease the fields need to be rotated every few years. Although if you are thinking green you do need to consider the question of air miles, as apart from a few states in the US who produce cane sugar, unless you live in the tropics it is invariably imported.

In common with most ethical decisions, it is a minefield and we leave it up to you to decide for yourself. As always, the quality of the end product is paramount but really when it comes to it, your jam will not taste any better from choosing one over the other. However as time-poor cooks ourselves (who isn't these days?) we tend to use cane as it sets much better; if you use beet sugar, your jam will take ages to make and will always be on the runny side.

Once you have decided, you need to identify your sugar du choix. In the United Kingdom, Tate and Lyle sugars are cane and Silver Spoon are beet. All Fairtrade sugar is cane sugar. In the United States there is no requirement to specify the source of the sugar on the label but truth in labelling legislation means that if it is labelled "pure cane sugar" it will be cane, otherwise it could be cane, beet or a mixture of the two.

Whether you use granulated or preserving, refined or unrefined is up to you. Preserving or jam sugar is usually more expensive than granulated. The individual grains of sugar are larger and this means they dissolve more easily, and this speeds up the whole process. It is good if, like us, you are impatient, but it doesn't make better jam. Using refined or unrefined sugar is entirely a matter of preference. We tend to use whatever we have to hand.

The next key point in jam making is determining the correct setting point. This is really not as daunting as it may seem at first.

The important thing to remember is, although you can always cook the jam a bit more, you cannot turn back time and it is crucial not to overcook jams and jellies as they become rubbery and may taste burnt. With this in mind always remove the pan from the heat whilst you test the jam to stop it cooking further. It does not matter how many times you do this, you can even recook cold jam if you decide it is not sufficiently set (or if you decide life is too short to continually reboil jam, just eat it a little runny, it will still taste fabulous and all will be fine, so long as you hold the toast level).

Testing whether the jam is set is very simple. Before you start your jam making put several saucers in the freezer. When you think the jam is almost ready, remove the pan from the heat and, using a teaspoon, put a small amount of jam on one of the cold saucers where it will rapidly cool. Push a clean finger through it and if it forms a wrinkly skin this means the jam is ready and will set when cooled. If it is ready, place it into the hot jars and leave to set. If it remains runny, return the pan to the heat and cook a little longer, then retest using another cold saucer. Do not forget to look in your freezer for any saucers you did not use, or else you will find one a month later, and wonder how it got there with nothing on it.

When cooking the jam, you will probably find a scum forming on the surface. If you scoop this off every time, you will end up wasting a lot of jam but with jam (as opposed to jelly) you can easily disperse the scum by adding a little butter. When you have determined that the correct setting point has been reached, put a knob of soft butter into the jam and stir till it melts and the scum will miraculously vanish. The amount of butter you need will depend on the quantity of jam and the prevalence of the scum, start with about ¼ teaspoon and add a little more if necessary.

Jelly making is a little different as the scum needs to be removed or it will spoil the clarity of the jelly. Once the jelly has reached setting point, allow it to cool slightly, then scoop off all the scum using a clean spoon. Although it doesn't look terribly attractive, it still tastes good and can be put in a separate jar and eaten by family.

It is important to sterilize your jars properly; otherwise you can run the risk of the jam going mouldy. If you are home alone it is perfectly safe to just spoon off any mould using a clean spoon and eat the jam beneath but obviously you don't want to give friends a jar of proudly made jam with a layer of blue mould. To sterilize, first preheat the oven to 110 C / 225 F / Gas ¼. Wash the jars and lids thoroughly in hot soapy water and rinse well or run them through a cycle of the dishwasher. Put the jars upside down in the oven and leave them until they are totally dry. If you are using metal lids they can go in the oven too. Drying the jars in the oven removes the risk of wiping them with a less than spotless cloth and also takes away the danger of a cold jar cracking when it meets hot jam.

When starting off your jam simmer the fruit slowly, to break it up and dissolve the sugar. Once the sugar has dissolved, bring to a rapid boil, as the quicker your jam reaches setting point the better the flavour will be.

Pectin levels in fruit affect the setting. Pectin levels vary from fruit to fruit: gooseberries and cranberries are high in pectin, whilst strawberries, blackberries and blueberries have low levels. Raspberries, loganberries, tayberries and boysenberries all have moderate amounts of pectin. Slightly under ripe fruit or those just on the point of ripeness will contain the highest levels of pectin and help your jam to set.

Finally, we prefer to make jams and jellies in small quantities (500 g / 1 lb to 1 kg / 2 lb). This ensures not only that you have a store cupboard full of variety and escape strawberry jam fatigue but also that the pan is not overloaded. Cooking the jam for a shorter time keeps the flavours clean and helps the fruit retain its shape.

STRAWBERRY AND ROSE JAM

Strawberry is the classic jam and an absolute must with scones or for filling a Victoria sandwich (we love it on hot buttered toast too). The following recipe gives a touch of Middle Eastern glamour with the addition of a little rosewater but if you prefer your jam classically pure, just leave it out.

A mixture of vanilla and strawberry ice cream (see page 130) piled up in a sundae dish, topped with whipped cream and some sliced strawberries and drizzled with a few tablespoons of the strawberry and rose jam is an absolute knockout pudding.

Makes 3 x 300 ml / 10 fl oz / 1 ¼ cup jars

750 g / 1 ½ lb firm strawberries
750 g / 1 ½ lb jam or preserving sugar
Juice of 1 ½ lemons
1 tablespoon of rosewater

Put your testing saucers in the freezer. Wash your jars thoroughly with soapy water, rinse and place in the oven on a very low heat to sterilize and warm the jars.

Halve or quarter any large berries and place in a preserving pan with the lemon juice. Bring up to a gentle simmer to let the strawberries release their juice. Simmer for 5 minutes. Add the sugar and stir to dissolve. Once dissolved bring the mixture up to a rolling boil and boil for 5 minutes. Test to see if it is ready. If not boil for another three minutes and test again.

Once the jam has reached setting point add a knob of butter and stir to dissolve any scum. Add the rosewater and stir in. Let it sit for 10 minutes to distribute the fruit and then put into the sterilized jars and seal. Label with the name and date. The jam will keep for a year.

GOOSEBERRY AND ELDERFLOWER JAM

This recipe is shamelessly lifted from Delia Smith's *Summer Collection.* You can absolutely trust a Delia recipe we always say. Jane made this three times in her great 2006 Jamfest and it remains a winner to this day.

Makes 3 x 450 g / 1 lb jars

900 g / 2 lb gooseberries, topped and tailed
900 g / 2 lb granulated sugar
150 ml / 5 fl oz water
4 tablespoons elderflower cordial
a trace of butter

Wash the jars in warm, soapy water, rinse well and leave to dry in a low oven.

Take a large, heavy saucepan and smear the bottom with butterpaper as this will help prevent the preserve from sticking at high temperatures. Add the gooseberries and water to the pan. Bring up to simmering point and simmer very gently until the fruit is soft, about 15 minutes.

Add the sugar and stir well. Wait until the sugar has dissolved completely, about 15 minutes. Turn the heat up and boil rapidly for 5-6 minutes, then take off the heat and test for set. If it is not ready then boil for a couple more minutes and test again and repeat until a spoonful on a chilled saucer wrinkles when you run your finger across it.

When ready, stir in the elderflower cordial and allow to settle for 15 minutes and pour into warm sterilized jars. Seal and label.

Spiced Port and Cranberry Jelly

This makes a lovely Christmas present and as a bonus goes really well with cold cuts of turkey and ham. The gentle spices are reminiscent of a Christmas punch. Make a batch in November for Christmas presents but remember to keep a jar or two back for yourself.

Makes 6 x 175 ml / 6 fl oz jars

1 kg / 2 lb Bramley (cooking) apples
350 g / 12 oz cranberries
300 ml / 10 fl oz / 1 ¼ cups of port or good red wine
1 tablespoon of whole cloves

2 small cinnamon sticks
3 star anise (plus extra to put in the jars)
zest and juice of an orange
granulated sugar

Chop the apples without peeling or coring them. Put in a large pan with the cranberries and 900 ml / 1 ½ pints / 3 ¾ cups cold water, the port or wine, the spices and the orange zest and juice. Bring to the boil, reduce the heat and simmer for 25 minutes stirring now and again. Do not crush the cranberries, as this will make the jelly cloudy.

Scald a large square of muslin in a pan of boiling water to sterilize (or you can use a new and non coloured jay cloth). Suspend this over a very large bowl, pour in the fruit mixture and leave to drip through until it stops. Don't squeeze the bag or rush it through with a spoon as this will make the jelly cloudy.

Return the pulp to the pan add another 600 ml / 1 pint / 2 ½ cups of water and simmer for a further 20 minutes. Drain through another square of muslin into a second bowl.

Combine the two juices and measure the volume. Allow 450 g / 16 oz / 2 ¼ cups sugar for each 600 ml / 1 pint of juice.

Pour the juice into a clean pan and bring to the boil and boil for 10 minutes. Add the sugar and stir till it has dissolved, then return to the boil and boil rapidly for 10 minutes. Test the jelly by putting a little onto a chilled saucer, push your finger across the surface if it wrinkles up, then it is ready. Otherwise boil for another 5 minutes and test again.

Remove from the heat and leave to settle for a couple of minutes. Remove any scum which has risen to the surface with a clean spoon. Ladle into sterilized jars, add a single star anise to each jar and leave for one hour – at this point you will need to poke the star anise down into the jelly with a skewer as it will have risen to the surface. Seal the jars and use within 3 months.

Gooseberry Curd

This is delicious on crumpets or use it in our Gooseberry Curd Cheesecake (see page 141). The recipe comes from Hugh Fearnley-Whittingstall who uses whole eggs in place of the more usual egg yolks. We think this makes a more stable curd. You can add a tablespoon of elderflower cordial to the curd at the end for a more floral taste if you like.

Makes 5 x 250 ml / 9 oz jars

500 g / 1 lb gooseberries, topped and tailed
100 ml / 3 ½ fl oz / ⅓ cup lemon juice
125 g / 4 oz / 1 stick of unsalted butter
450 g / 16 oz / 2 ¼ cups granulated sugar
200 ml / 7 fl oz strained beaten egg (about 4-5 eggs but do measure it)

Sterilize your jam jars as outlined above.

Put the gooseberries in a pan with the lemon juice. Bring just up to the boil stirring and simmer for 5-10 minutes or until the fruit has collapsed. Run through a sieve to get a smooth purée.

Put the purée, butter and sugar in a large basin over a pan of boiling water. Stir until the butter has melted and the mixture is smooth. Take off the heat and let cool for a minute (too hot will scramble the eggs, the mixture should be cool enough to comfortably put a finger in it). Add the strained beaten eggs, whisking the whole time. Return to the heat and continue to stir until the mixture thickens, this will take 10-15 minutes. You must stir this constantly and watch the heat as too hot and the whole thing will scramble. Once the curd is the consistency of home-made mayonnaise, put into the warm jars and seal. Use within a month and keep opened jars in the fridge for up to a week.

Hemsley and Hemsley's Blueberry Chia Jam

This is not really a jam as such but it is an easy and quick breakfast preserve, which is terrifically good for you with its mix of antioxidant berries and superfood chia seeds. It comes from Jasmine and Melissa Hemsley's book *The Art of Eating Well*, an absolute bible of delicious healthy eating. The chia seeds when mixed with liquid have a slightly glutinous texture which "sets" the jam. Because there is no sugar to preserve this, keep it in the fridge and use within a week.

Makes 1 400 g / 14 oz jar

175 g / 6 oz blueberries
1 ½ tablespoons chia seeds
1 – 2 tablespoons honey
lemon juice to taste

Mash the berries or blend in a food processor. Mix in the chia seeds, the honey and 1 tablespoon of warm water. Stir well to stop clumps forming and put into the jar. Put into the fridge to set for at least an hour. Taste and add more honey or a little lemon juice to taste.

Raspberry Vinegar

You can make this with blackberries, mulberries or brambles but we make it most often with raspberries as we like to have some on hand for the totally delicious raspberry vinaigrette (see page 172). This will keep about 6 months.

Makes 500 ml / 16 fl oz

250 g / 8 oz raspberries
60 g / 2 oz / 4 tablespoons caster (superfine) sugar
400 ml / 14 fl oz / 1 ¼ cups red wine vinegar

Put the berries, sugar and vinegar into a saucepan and heat gently stirring occasionally until the sugar has dissolved and the juices are starting to run (10 –15 minutes). Leave to cool overnight. Strain and discard the fruit and put the vinegar into clean sterilized bottles.

HEDGEROW KETCHUP

A tangy sauce which goes beautifully with steak and sausages or even in your morning bacon sandwich. Add the chipotle if you like a stronger chilli kick.

Makes about 500 ml / 1 pint

500 g / 1 lb elderberries
500 g / 1 lb blackberries, brambles or mulberries or a mix
3 shallots, finely diced
2 teaspoons salt
300 ml / 10 fl oz / 1 ¼ cups red wine vinegar
2 tablespoons grated fresh ginger
1 teaspoon English mustard powder
1 teaspoon of chipotle paste (optional)
1 cinnamon stick
1 teaspoon ground allspice
2 teaspoons dried chilli flakes (or to taste)
freshly ground black pepper
250 g / 8 oz / 1 cup dark brown soft sugar

Wash your bottles well in hot soapy water, rinse and leave to dry in a very low oven.

Strip the elderberries off of the stalks. We find the easiest was to do this is with a fork. Do it over a bowl as the elderberry juice will stain. Put the fruit, shallots, salt and vinegar into a large pan. Add the spices and stir well. Bring slowly up to the boil, then reduce the heat and simmer for 30 minutes until the fruit is softened. If you like your sauces very smooth, push through a sieve (strainer) and return to the cleaned pan. We tend to just give it a quick whiz with the stick blender which leads to a sauce you dollop rather than pour.

Add the sugar to the fruit mixture in the pan and bring up to the boil, stirring to dissolve the sugar. Boil hard for 10-12 minutes or until thickened and syrupy. Pour into the clean warm bottles and seal and label.

RUMTOPF

A Rumtopf is a project as much as a recipe, taking many months to come to readiness but it is so worth the wait. It is a traditional German Christmas treat served over vanilla ice cream. Spoonfuls of the preserving liquor are great topped up with sparkling wine (champagne if you can) for a heady Christmas cocktail. A Rumtopf packs a real punch and is definitely only for grown-ups.

Basically fruit are added to the traditional crockpot gradually as each comes into season, topping up with sugar and rum as you go. Ideal fruit for a Rumtopf are strawberries, cherries, apricots, plums, blackberries and raspberries.

Because this is a long slow process it is absolutely essential that your fruit are in tiptop condition with absolutely no mould or bruising, and that you start with a sterile jar,

It will make as much as it makes, depending on how many layers of fruit you put in.

Start in the summer when the berry season starts. You need a small lidded crock or ceramic jar with a volume of about 2-3 litres / 3 ½ - 5 pints.

Make sure the crock is thoroughly clean and dry. Start it off with 400 g / 14 oz with your first fruit (we like to start with strawberries, hulled but kept whole) and sprinkle with 200 g / 7 oz of sugar. Cover the fruit and sugar with rum. Put cling film (saran wrap) over the top of the crock and put on the lid. Keep in a cool, dark place.

Each time a new fruit comes into season, open the crock, put the fruit in, add more sugar and more rum. For stone fruit like apricots and plums stone and halve them, pit the cherries. Add 400 g / 14 oz fruit and 200 g / 7 oz sugar each time and make sure everything is completely covered with the rum. Once the last fruit has been added, leave alone until Christmas.

RUMTOPF TRIFLE

This is an ideal use for the fruit and juices from your rumtopf project (see page 203). It makes a most delicious and very boozy trifle. Make this in a pretty crystal bowl so you can see the layers. You can make your own Madeira cake if you like but a good quality bought one is fine once soaked in all that boozy fruit and saves a lot of time.

Serves 4-6

250 g / 8 oz of fruit from your rumtopf (you can just do one layer for a single fruit or dig deep for a delightful mixture, just make sure you get plenty of berries)
125 ml / 4 fl oz / ½ cup juice from the rumtopf
1 Madeira cake
150 ml / 5 fl oz / ⅔ cup full fat milk
200 ml / 7 fl oz / ¾ cup double cream
6 egg yolks
1 tablespoon caster (superfine) sugar
1 teaspoon vanilla essence (extract)
1 tablespoon caster (superfine) sugar
300 ml / ½ pint / 1 ½ cups double cream
Raspberry pearl to decorate (optional)

First make the custard. Bring the milk and cream just up to boiling point. Whisk the egg yolks, vanilla and sugar till light and fluffy. Pour over the milk and cream mixture and beat to combine. Return to the pan and keeping the heat very low stir continuously until thickened and the custard coats the back of a spoon. Do not be tempted to turn up the heat to hurry this along you will only scramble the eggs and ruin the custard. Set aside to cool.

Cut the sponge into chunky 5 cm / 2 in cubes and layer in the bottom of a serving bowl. Pour over the boozy juices from the rumtopf and let sit for 10 minutes or so to absorb. Cover with the fruit itself.

Whip the cream with sugar to soft peaks. Do not over whip. Dollop over the whipped cream. Scatter the surface liberally with raspberry pearls. If you don't have the pearls then scatter with a few fresh berries.

If you can wait, this benefits from a sitting in the fridge for a couple of hours to let the flavours meld.

BERRY BUTTER

This is delicious on freshly baked scones. It is best served directly from the fridge. If you make a batch, what you don't eat can be formed into a log wrapped well in cling film (saran wrap) and frozen. Defrost before use.

Makes 275 g / 9 oz

250 g / 8 oz / 2 sticks unsalted butter
2 tablespoons icing (confectioners') sugar, sifted
seeds from one vanilla pod or ½ tsp vanilla extract
90 g / 3 oz of strawberries (4-5 large ones), hulled and finely chopped

Beat the butter, sugar and vanilla seeds for five minutes until softened. Add the berries and beat to combine. Use immediately or store in the fridge.

Berry Drinks

Cranberry Vodka

One year we made this as a Christmas present for the girls in our bookgroup and it was very well received. It is a beautifully festive colour and packaged in pretty glass bottles makes a lovely gift. Use it to make a Christmas cocktail (a shot of cranberry vodka in the bottom of a flute topped up with Prosecco) or in place of cherry brandy to spike the cranberry sauce on page 184.

Makes 1 litre

250 g / 8 oz fresh cranberries
1 litre / 1 ¾ pints / 4 cups vodka
175 g / 6 oz / ¾ cup caster (superfine) sugar

Prick your cranberries with a sterile darning needle or skewer and layer up with the sugar in a large sterilized jar or wide mouthed bottle and pour over the vodka. Shake thoroughly. Keep in a cool place for 2 weeks shaking well every day. After two weeks strain through clean muslin and bottle. Keeps for at least a year.

Mulled Apple and Cranberry Punch

This is a warming and delicious drink for a bonfire party, positively autumnal it will get your guests in the mood for the sparklers. We really recommend using a single varietal apple juices, it will make all the difference.

(Serves 6-8)

750 ml / 1 ½ pints cider
750 ml / 1 ½ pints apple juice
750 ml / 1 ½ pints cranberry juice

½ cup dried cranberries
150 ml / ¼ pint sloe gin
2 cinnamon sticks
3 cloves

Put all the ingredients into a large saucepan and heat gently over a low to medium heat. You want this to come to just below simmering point so it is comfortingly warming but on no account boil it.

Pimms

When Sally went canal boating with some friends one summer, this was the drink du jour everyday at Pimms o'clock. Pimms is the quintessential English summer drink and strawberries are essential to the perfect mix. If it is raining, as sadly it so often is in an English summer, do feel free to add a cocktail parasol to prevent the raindrops falling in your drink.

Makes a large jug of Pimms enough for 6-8 people

400 ml / 14 fl oz / 1 ¾ c Pimms no. 1
1 bottle / 750 ml / 25 fl oz lemonade or soda water
1 bottle / 750 ml / 25 fl oz ginger ale
½ cucumber
8-10 strawberries, hulled and halved
2-3 sprigs of fresh mint
ice cubes

Mix together the liquids in a pretty glass jug or punch bowl. Run a vegetable peeler down the sides of the cucumber to make long ribbons (keep the peel on) and add these, the strawberries and mint sprigs to the jug or punch bowl with ice.

Raspberry Lemonade

This is a delicately pink drink perfect for summer picnics. It also makes a great granita. Just pour into a shallow tray, freeze for an hour, take out and break up the crystals with a fork. Repeat three or four more times over the next few hours until you have a delicious pile of sweetly pink icy shards.

If you prefer your lemonade a little more sparkling, then follow the recipe as below but use only one cup of water. This will give you a cordial base which will keep well in the fridge for up to a week. When ready to serve pour a little into individual glasses and top up with sparkling mineral water or club soda.

Makes a quart or a large jug

675 ml / 1 ½ pints / 3 cups cold water
50 g / 1 ¾ oz / ¼ cup, plus 1 tablespoon golden caster (superfine) sugar
140 g / 5 oz / 1 cup raspberries
250 ml / 9 fl oz / 1 cup lemon juice plus the zest of the lemons

Combine the water and the sugar (reserving the extra tablespoon), heat gently stirring to dissolve the sugar. Cool. Combine the raspberries with the remaining tablespoon of sugar and leave to macerate whilst the syrup cools. Whizz the raspberries in a blender and pass through a sieve (strainer) to remove the seeds. Add the raspberry purée and the lemon juice and zest to the syrup. Mix and chill. Serve over ice.

Louy's Elderflower Cordial

Collecting elderflowers is one of the signs that summer is on the way. Jane's friend Louy lives near a brilliant (but secret) park, which is edged with elder trees. Every year the phone call comes, Jane leaps into the car with her foraging baskets and, two days later, they have perfect cordial. This recipe is incredibly easy, but the quality of the cordial depends on the flower heads. They should be fully open and fluffy, but not going over. Avoid any that are brown or dry as they will spoil the flavour. Pick above waist level and avoid trees on busy roads.

This will keep for a year frozen in small plastic bottles and Jane and Louy always say they will make our annual supply, but somehow it is never quite enough.

Makes 2 x 750 ml / 1 ½ pint bottles

20 large elderflower heads
600 ml / 1 pint / 2 ½ cups boiling water
875 g / 2 lbs /4 ½ cups granulated sugar
2 lemons, rind grated and then sliced
50 g citric acid

Dissolve the sugar in the boiling water. Remove the pan from the heat and add the elderflowers, grated lemon rind, sliced lemons and citric acid. Leave the mixture to steep for 24 to 36 hours.

Strain through muslin and pour into pretty bottles. Dilute the cordial to taste, with either still or sparkling water. It will keep for 2-3 weeks.

The cordial can be frozen in small bottles and will last for up to a year. Remember to leave a little space in the bottle to allow for expansion when the liquid freezes.

STRAWBERRY DAQUIRI

The classic berry cocktail.

Makes 1

4 fresh strawberries, hulled, plus ½ strawberry to garnish
2 teaspoons white sugar

35 ml / 1½ fl oz white rum
1 tablespoon strawberry liqueur
25 ml / 1 fl oz lime juice

Place the strawberries, sugar, rum, strawberry liqueur and lime juice into the base of a cocktail shaker and mash (muddle) with the end of a clean rolling pin.

Place the lid onto the cocktail shaker and shake well. Strain the mixture into a Martini glass and garnish with half a strawberry.

Scarlett O'Hara

This classic cocktail was reputedly created in 1939 to celebrate the opening of what must be one of the greatest movies of all time and one of our all-time favourites. It is sweet and tart (just like us). You can make this by the glass or scale up and make a jug. Frankly my dear, we do give a damn.

1 part Southern Comfort
1 part fresh lime juice
2 parts cranberry juice
a lime wedge to garnish
granulated sugar to frost the glass

Dampen the rim of a cocktail glass and stand in a saucer of sugar to create a frosted rim. Pour the Southern Comfort, lime juice and cranberry juice into a shaker with ice, and shake well. Strain into the glass and serve.

Sloe Gin

This is the forager's favourite tipple and it makes a beautiful pink coloured G&T. The recipe comes from Sally's Uncle David who was a keen home brewer.

Makes 900 ml / 1 ½ pints

500 g / 1 lb sloes
750 ml / 1 ½ pints of gin
100 g / 3 ½ oz white granulated sugar

Make sure your sloes are in tip top condition, discarding any bruised or mouldy ones. Prick the sloes with a silver or stainless steel fork or skewer. Place in a large china or glass bowl and pour on the gin (wash out the bottle and keep this to store your sloe gin later). Stir in the sugar. Cover tightly with cling film (saran wrap) and leave in a cool dark place for 2-3 months.

Strain through muslin and pour back into the reserved bottle. Seal and leave to mature. This will taste better after a year and keep up to 4 years.

GLOSSARY

ACID: soil with a pH of less than 7.

ALKALINE: soil with a pH of more than 7.

BARE-ROOTED: plants sold during their dormant season without soil around their roots.

BLETTED: a process most associated with medlars, this allows a fruit to ripen to the point where it begins to rot. Some rowans need to be bletted to become palatable.

CHELATES: organic compounds which enable plants to take up elements which would otherwise be trapped in the soil. Manganese and iron, in particular, are insoluble in high-lime soils and plants can suffer from a deficiency, resulting in lime-induced chlorosis of the leaves.

CORDON AND DOUBLE CORDON: a plant (usually a fruit tree or bush) pruned and trained to a single stem. Double or U cordons have two stems.

CULTIVAR: a variety within a species, cultivated by man. These are frequently (and wrongly) called varieties.

DRUPE AND COMPOUND DRUPE: a fruit consisting of one or more hard seeds or stones surrounded by a fleshy outer covering, e.g. sloes. Compound drupes consist of a number of drupelets, e.g. blackberry.

DRUPELET: a small drupe, usually part of composite fruit, e.g. blackberry.

ERICACEOUS: plants that will not tolerate lime in the soil and need a pH of 6.5 or less. It is also used to describe the compost which is suitable for these plants.

FALSE FRUIT: botanically these are called accessory fruits, as some or all of the flesh is not derived from the ovary. Strawberries are compound false fruits; the pips on the surface being the true fruits.

FAMILY: the category of plant classification which includes a group of related genera. It is botanically important but is not usually given on horticultural labels.

FAN: the stems of the plant are spread out against a support, typically a fence or wall, and trained into a fan shape by pruning and tying-in.

GENUS (plural genera): the category of plant classification between family and species. It is based on the plant's botanical characteristics and is indicated by its first Latin name.

HARDWOOD CUTTING: a method of propagating deciduous plants from woody stems. The cuttings should be taken in autumn after the leaves have fallen. The cuttings should be taken in the same way as softwood ones (see below), with stems 30 cm / 12 in long, cut just below a bud. They can take up to a year to root. Gooseberries, goji berries and honeyberries can be propagated using hardwood cuttings.

HEELED IN: temporarily planted until the plant can be put in its final position.

HYBRID: the offspring of plants of two different species or genera.

LATERAL: side-shoot growing off the main stem.

LAYERING: a method of propagation whereby a shoot grows its own root system and can be cut from the main plant to produce a separate one. Self-layering occurs naturally. Blackberries, hybrid brambles and strawberries can be propagated by layering.

pH: this refers to the acidity or alkalinity of the soil. pH 7 is neutral, above is alkaline, below is acid.

POWDERY MILDEW: a fungus whose powdery spores make the leaves of the plant appear white. Certain plants are more susceptible than others and resistant varieties are increasingly available. Keep the soil well watered and mulched and avoid using nitrogenous fertilizer as this encourages soft growth.

PROPAGATING: making new plants from seeds, cuttings, layering or division.

RUNNER: a shoot which grows low along the ground and can often be used to make a new plant.

SELF-FERTILE: a plant whose flowers can self-pollinate, i.e. a flower which can be pollinated by its own pollen, or by that from another flower on the same plant.

SEQUESTERED: see chelates, above.

SOFTWOOD CUTTING: a method of propagating from soft stems. Select a healthy shoot and take a cutting 10 cm / 4 in long, cutting just below a leaf joint. Trim away the lower leaves, put into a pot of suitable potting compost and keep well watered. They will root faster if you dip the stems in hormone rooting powder and put them in a propagator or cover the pot with a plastic bag to prevent evaporation. Blueberries, goji berries and honeyberries can be propagated using softwood cuttings.

SPECIES (sp. plural spp.): the category of classification below genus consisting of botanically closely related plants. The species is indicated by the plant's second Latin name.

SUBSPECIES (subsp. or ssp. plural subspp.): a subdivision of species, this can be further divided into individual varieties (var.).

'THREE Ds': dead, diseased and damaged branches

USDA ZONES: United States Department of Agriculture zones which are based on the average annual minimum temperatures and indicate in which areas a plant will thrive.

VARIETY (var.): a smaller group of plants within a species.

BIBLIOGRAPHY

THE STORY OF BERRIES

Brears, Peter, *Cooking and Dining in Tudor and Early Stuart England,* Prospect Books, 2015

Davidson, Alan, *The Oxford Companion to Food,* Oxford University Press, 2014

Grigson, Geoffrey, *The Englishman's Flora,* Phoenix House, 1958

Mason, Laura, *The Taste of Britain,* Harper Press, 2006

Mabey, Richard, *Flora Britannica,* Sinclair-Stevenson, 1996

Palter, Robert, *The Duchess of Malfi's Apricots and Other Literary Fruits,* University of South Carolina Press, 2002

Potter, Jennifer, *Strange Blooms, the Curious Lives and Adventures of the John Tradescants,* Atlantic Books, 2006

Reich, Lee, *Uncommon Fruits Worthy of Attention,* Addison-Wesley Publishing Company, 1991

Roach, F. A. *The Cultivated Fruits of Britain,* Blackwell, 1985

Roberts, Jonathan, *Cabbages and Kings: the Origins of Fruit and Vegetables,* HarperCollins, 2001

Ryley, Claire, *Roman Gardens and their Plants,* Sussex Archaeological Society, 1998

BERRIES FOR HEALTH

Neal's Yard Remedies: Healing Foods, edited by Susannah Steel, Dorling Kindersley, 2013

Blythman, Joanna, *What To Eat: Food that's Good for Your Health, Pocket and Plate,* Fourth Estate, 2013

Pollan, Michael, *In Defence of Food: The Myth of Nutrition and the Pleasure of Eating,* Penguin, 2009

Wills, Judith, *The Food Bible,* Quadrille, 2007

BERRIES IN THE HEDGEROW

These are a mixture of practical guides and inspiring reads. When foraging in a new area find fellow foragers and ask which local guide books they find best.

Génevé, Alain and Marie-Jeanne, *Wild Fruit: A Field Guide to Britain and Europe,* Timber Press, 2014

Gibbons, Euell, *Stalking the Wild Asparagus,* David McKay Company, 1962

Irving, Miles, *The Forager Handbook,* Ebury Press, 2009

Lewis–Stempel, John, *Foraging: The Essential Guide to Free Wild Food,* Right Way, 2012

Lewis–Stempel, John, *The Wild Life: A Year of Living on Wild Food,* Black Swan, 2010

Mabey, Richard, *Food for Free: A Guide to the Edible Wild Plants of Britain,* Collins, 1972

Phillips, Roger, *Wild Food: A Complete Guide for Foragers,* Macmillan, 2014

Squire, David, *Self-Sufficiency: Foraging,* New Holland Publishers, 2011

Thoreau, Henry David, *Walden or Life in the Woods,* Everyman's Library, J.M. Dent, 1908

Thoreau, Henry David, *Wild Fruits,* W.W. Norton and Company, 2000

Wright, John, *River Cottage Handbook No.7: Hedgerow,* Bloomsbury, 2010

BERRIES IN THE GARDEN

The Royal Horticultural Society A-Z Encyclopedia of Garden Plants, editor-in-chief Christopher Brickell, Dorling Kindersley, 2008

Abbott, Marylyn, *Gardens of Plenty: the Art of the Potager Garden,* Kyle Cathie Limited, 2001

Diacono, Mark, *A Taste of the Unexpected,* Quadrille Publishing Limited, 2010

Diacono, Mark, *The New Kitchen Garden,* Saltyard Books, 2015

Diacono, Mark, *River Cottage Handbook No 9: Fruit,* Bloomsbury, 2011
Don, Monty and Sarah, *Fork to Fork,* Conran Octopus, 1999
Flowerdew, Bob, *Complete Fruit Book,* Kyle Cathie Limited, 1995
McMorland Hunter, Jane, *The Tiny Garden,* Frances Lincoln, 2006
McMorland Hunter, Jane and Kelly, Chris, *For the Love of an Orchard,* Pavilion, 2010
McMorland Hunter, Jane and Kelly, Chris, *Teach Yourself Basic Gardening,* Hodder Educational, 2010
Books by the following on berries, and indeed all fruit and vegetables, are inspiring and informative: Alan Buckingham, Alys Fowler, Dr D.G. Hessayon, Carol Klein and Alan Titchmarsh.

HISTORICAL COOKERY AND GARDENING BOOKS AND HERBALS

Beeton's Book of Household Management, edited by Mrs Isabella Beeton, a facsimile of the first edition of 1861, Southover Press, 1996
Culpeper, Nicholas, *The Complete Herbal,* Harvey Sales, 1981
De Mauduit, Vicomte, *They Can't Ration These,* Persephone Books, 2004
Evelyn, John, *John Evelyn, Cook,* edited by Christopher Driver, Prospect Books, 1997
Evelyn, John, *Directions for the Gardiner and other Horticultural Advice,* edited by Maggie Campbell-Culver, Oxford University Press, 2009
Gerard, John, *Leaves from Gerard's Herball,* arranged by Marcus Woodward, The Bodley Head, 1931
Hill, Thomas, *The Gardener's Labyrinth,* edited by Richard Mabey, Oxford University Press, 1987
Nott, John, *The Cooks and Confectioners Dictionary: Or, the Accomplish'd Housewives Companion,* Introduction and Glossary by Elizabeth David, Lawrence Rivington, 1980
Pliny the Elder, *Natural History,* translated by John F. Healey, Penguin Books, 1991
Tusser, Thomas, *Five Hundred Points of Good Husbandry,* Oxford University Press, 1984

BERRIES IN THE KITCHEN

Books for Cooks Volumes 1-10, Pryor Publications, 2001 onwards

Bunyard, Edward, *The Anatomy of Dessert*, Modern Library, 2006

Clay, Xanthe, *It's Raining Plums,* John Murray, 2002

Fearnley-Whittingstall, Hugh, *River Cottage Fruit Every Day,* Bloomsbury, 2013

Granger, Bill, *Sydney Food,* Murdoch Books, 2009

Grigson, Jane, *Jane Grigson's Fruit Book,* Penguin Books, 2000

Harris, Joanne, and Warde, Fran, *The French Kitchen,* Doubleday, 2002

Hemsley, Jasmine and Melissa, *The Art of Eating Well,* Ebury Press, 2014

Lawson, Nigella, *Nigella's Christmas,* Chatto and Windus, 2008

Medrich, Alice, *Chocolat,* Warner Books, 1990

Slater, Nigel, *Tender, Volume II,* Fourth Estate, 2010

Smith, Delia, *Summer Collection,* BBC Books, 1993

Smith, Delia, *Book of Cakes,* Book Club Associates, 1978

Spaull, Susan, *Ideal Home Entertaining,* Boxtree Limited, 1999

Spaull, Susan, *Leiths Techniques Bible*, Bloomsbury, 2003

Waters, Alice, *Chez Panisse Fruit,* HarperCollins, 2002

Wheatley, Jo, *Home Baking,* Constable, 201

ACKNOWLEDGEMENTS

We would like to thank the following:

Wendy and Kerri-Anne Hughes for help with recipe testing.

Everyone at Hatchards for their discerning tasting of the results, and for being so tolerant and supportive of the author in their midst.

Ian Taylor, who would like our next book to be on beef.

Louy Piachaud for her elderflower cordial recipe.

The staff at the Library at RHS Wisley; this is a delightful library to use as it is situated in a beautiful garden with lots of berries.

Sue and David Gibb, Jane's foraging companions, who braved thorns and purple juice stains, and Euan Macdonald for his advice.

Patricia Hughes for help with proofing.

Paul at P. Cooper and Sons, our favourite Twickenham greengrocer, who found us beautiful berries when the garden couldn't keep up with the recipe testing.

Teresa Chris, our agent, who guided the book through its early stages.

Catheryn Kilgarriff at Prospect Books whose enthusiasm for berries equalled our own and who kept us supplied with haskaps from Haskapa Haskap Products.

Finally, all our friends and family for enjoying, and at times enduring, berries with everything.

INDEX

Many of the fruits have a bracket following which gives the main name we have used for the fruit e.g. blaeberry (see bilberry). For reasons of space, not all common names are listed.

All recipes are listed alphabetically by the berry under RECIPES. General cooking techniques are listed in the main alphabet.